LEADERSHIP SKILLS FOR NEW AND SEASONED MANAGERS

BUILD SELF-CONFIDENCE FAST WITH 21 TOP TIPS YOU CAN IMPLEMENT TODAY TO CREATE AN EMPOWERED, HIGHLY EFFECTIVE WORKPLACE.

RIGOBERTO COLMENARES NUNEZ

❀ Created with Vellum

CONTENTS

INTRODUCTION

Humans are inherently social creatures, as meeting even the most basic of needs requires the help of others. Networking, teamwork, and shared objectives are therefore implicit in every aspect of social life. Because of this, modern societies have evolved into complex macrosystems of various institutions to meet everyone's requirements. More complex civilizations have more specialized institutions with more nuanced goals and more complex networks of interdependence.

This level of complexity calls for an in-depth familiarity with the context, an overview of the desired outcomes, strategic application of available resources, and careful orchestration of all the moving pieces. The key to being successful in all of these endeavors is good management.

Management in contemporary society is the driving force behind the success of groups and organizations. Management may most commonly be linked with the commercial or manufacturing sectors. Still, it is essential to the success of any group or company. An organization's fate can hinge on the choices made by its management. No matter how big or small an organization is, even if it's just one person or a small team, everyone must rely on management to succeed.

Being a manager is a full-time job, so managers often have to put off furthering their education in favor of dealing with urgent matters. However, the world is constantly changing, and businesses must adapt to the simultaneous motion of many factors.

This convoluted situation raises more questions than answers for the involved businesses. That is why it's so important for managers to have crystal-clear mental models of their operations. Theorizing again is a helpful technique for analyzing managerial efficacy and team dynamics. Any manager, leader, or person in charge of a team, organization, or process will benefit from this book's compilation of fundamental concepts and best practices.

Everyone, especially those in positions of authority, must constantly improve their knowledge and abilities to keep up with the changing world. In this "Leadership Skills for New and Seasoned Managers" guide, I have outlined the essential ideas to remember and the abilities you'll need to become an effective manager in the modern era.

For as long as I can remember, we should all have access to a reference book as we move into new stages of our professional (and personal) lives. I decided to write this book because I felt obligated to share the insights I've gained from life with others. I wanted to share what I've learned with others so they wouldn't have to make the same mistakes I did. Because, ultimately, if people who follow in our footsteps have to learn the same things we did—on their own—how can we expect them to be more successful than we were?

Anyone in a position of authority over others should have formal instruction in management and supervision techniques. This book will lead you on a journey of self-discovery and skill development. A combination of supervisory and management abilities is required to effectively direct and monitor team members to ensure they adhere to organizational policies and procedures. The presence of one guarantees the presence of the other. When you're in charge of supervising a group of people, you're also in charge of managing the people-related aspects of the workplace, and vice versa.

Those in positions of authority must possess the indispensable skills of management and supervision. Promotion applicants and current employees alike would greatly benefit from preparatory and continuous training, and any company that does so would be doing its customers and shareholders a favor. Suppose the company needs to be more thoughtless to provide this training. In that case, those aspiring to leadership roles should do so independently.

I would wager that genuinely successful organizations have trained and encouraged their employees to go above and beyond to meet their daily missions while also clearly stating and pursuing their visions and ultimately achieving those visions, whereas in most organizations, simply being a good supervisor and manager is enough to "get by."

From what I've seen over the years, the most efficient, effective, and successful organizations are the ones that invest heavily in their people by not only teaching and reinforcing supervisory and management skills but also by teaching and encouraging their supervisors and managers to become influential leaders.

I am well aware that this is not the first book on supervision and management, and it is most certainly not the first on leadership. However, I do believe that what I offer is unique in that what I present is neither theory nor philosophy but rather a compilation of simple, well-known concepts that have actually worked for me.

While I am an enthusiastic supporter of furthering your education in the topics covered in this book, my primary motivation for producing it is to help you and your organization establish a solid footing from which to grow and succeed.

The layout of the book is purposefully straightforward to follow. The readers of this book are public and private sector supervisors and managers who want to learn and grow in their positions, as well as those who want to understand the value of being a good leader who cares for the people over whom they have authority.

As your former supervisor, manager, and leader, I am responsible for passing this information along to all of you in the hopes that it will help you grow professionally and personally. In return, I expect you to be an even better supervisor, manager, and leader than I was and that you will pass these lessons on to those who will follow in your footsteps. Here are some of the ways you will benefit from reading this book:

- To realize your full potential if you struggle with self-awareness and self-evaluation.
- To become an inclusive and conscious leader if you need help managing a diverse workforce.
- To become an excellent communicator if you have problems conveying your expectations and needs to your teams or resolving conflicts at work.
- To keep up with your work's lofty goals and stringent expectations, this book can give you the drive you need to get there.
- To become a successful leader in difficult situations if you feel worried and exhausted at work and believe it affects your leadership skills.
- This manual is for you if you're a leader who wants to see the people on your team succeed but need to know where to start.
- This book will teach you how to link your team and the rest of the organization so that you can help them reach their full business potential.

Leadership entails inspiring, motivating, and trusting followers to achieve the aims. In contrast, management involves planning and organization to realize those goals. Sharing a vision for a better future and inspiring your team to work toward it with the plans, procedures, and tasks you established as a manager is closely tied to your ability to achieve results.

A great leader can get the team to see the big picture, but it takes an even better manager to get each member to feel like they are contributing to that picture. Both leadership and management require you to be proactive and creative. Still, management requires you to be directive, action-oriented, and responsive.

Your ability to establish yourself as an effective leader depends on how well you apply the management skills you've learned in this guide. The best leaders are always open to new ideas and information because they realize that their current level of knowledge is minimal compared to the amount they have yet to acquire.

Leaders who aren't afraid to take the blame, take risks, and make decisions when it counts tend to be the most admired by their followers. For a good reason: their bravery, wit, and fortitude impress and reassure the masses, making them eager to follow in their footsteps. Excellent management relies on strong leadership. I'll cover that topic and share some of my best insider secrets.

By presenting the strategies used by the most successful leaders to create a culture where people want to be there and have a sense of pride and ownership over their work, this book aims to teach aspiring, newly appointed, and experienced managers or business owners how to develop the skills to become an empathetic leader rather than a disconnected manager. If you want to succeed in life and business, you need to learn how to build and sustain a high-performing team culture, and this book will show you how.

CHAPTER 1
THE GREAT QUALITIES OF LEADERS

Many businesses failed because they needed help to keep up with rivals worldwide. Even if some were initially successful, the vast majority eventually failed. Leaders like Steve Jobs, Elon Musk, and Warren Buffet have advanced their organizations through innovative thinking, dogged perseverance, and luck. They brought a new point of view to the business sector with their conviction and boldness as leaders. A skilled leader will showcase qualities like honesty, self-awareness, courage, respect, empathy, and gratitude. It's important for them to educate themselves in adaptable techniques, boosting their impact while enhancing communication and delegation. Take a closer look at how these vital leadership skills can be imparted and fostered throughout your organization.

Qualities of a Leader that Make for a Great Leader

A skilled leader possesses the prowess to inspire their team through interpersonal finesse and tackle challenges with technical acumen. Unearthing the qualities that set exceptional leaders apart can serve as a compass for your own leadership journey. As you embark on this enlightening exploration, we'll delve into the 20 defining characteristics that encapsulate the essence of an effective leader. These characteristics, each laden with simple meanings, provide the common language through which we'll converse about the attributes of great leadership. My mission is to guide you in nurturing these traits within yourself, laying the foundation for what lies ahead in our journey of leadership discovery.

Accountability: Leaders must own up to their team and blunders, apologize sincerely, and endeavor to improve processes and procedures moving forward. For leaders to succeed, this is a must.

Active listening: Leaders who excel at giving and receiving team feedback can eliminate distractions, pay attention to nonverbal signs, and paraphrase what others have said. Reducing background noise, paying attention to nonverbal gestures, and making brief notes can all help.

Collaboration: Leaders must work internally and externally to identify shared objectives and form relationships to yield the best possible results for everyone involved. For goals to be aligned and expectations to be understood, people involved in collaboration must prioritize open lines of communication.

Courage: Successful leaders have the guts to do what's best for their employees and enterprises. They can also demonstrate bravery by challenging themselves to develop new abilities or take on additional tasks.

Communication: As a team, you will succeed if each member can convey their wants and goals and listen to others. As a result, they can better articulate their needs, wants, and aspirations.

Empathy: Influential leaders demonstrate empathy when they take the time to understand their staff's perspectives and experiences, strengthening working relationships. Being empathetic as a leader is crucial.

Flexibility: A flexible CEO can continue to guide an organization through unforeseen challenges. They will try novel approaches if they believe they will benefit the group or company. Being flexible and adaptable is a highly sought-after trait in a prospective employee.

Focus: An intelligent leader creates a workable vision and establishes reasonable, attainable goals. They are adept at SMART goal setting, which requires detailed, quantifiable, achievable, relevant, and timely objectives. Using the SMART goal-setting framework to set yourself up for success.

Growth mindset: Leaders must cultivate a growth mentality to adjust to new information and maintain momentum. They need a growth mentality and be flexible in the face of technological and personal shifts.

Eager to learn: Leaders that keep up with the latest developments in their fields, use that knowledge to sharpen their abilities, and encourage their teams to do the same are highly influential. Motivating the team to invest in their learning is possible through a commitment to continued education or participation in professional development initiatives.

Innovation: Influential leaders foster an innovative and creative culture by providing opportunities for brainstorming, prototyping, and listening to and inspiring their staff to think outside the box.

Optimism: Leaders who are optimistic about the future of their company recognize the importance of their employees' efforts and reward them accordingly. They anticipate problems, keep an upbeat attitude, and help the team when things get tough.

Passion: A leader's belief in their work's importance and apparent interest in it will inspire their team and help them achieve their shared goals. The result may be more enthusiastic and dedicated employees.

Patience: Leaders who can help their teams overcome mistakes made in the workplace exhibit patience. Patience entails realizing blunders are inevitable, letting them go, and moving on. They might also be patient when teaching workers how to perform new tasks.

Problem-solving: Influential leaders understand the value of teaching their teams to think critically and creatively when facing challenges.

Resilience: Leaders have keen insight and are resilient enough to initiate new procedures, recruit fresh talent, or alter long-established norms. They are result-oriented, can tune out the noise, and set the pace.

Respect: The best leaders show their team's appreciation and listen to their input. These leaders inspire loyalty and pride in their work by giving workers autonomy in decision-making and encouraging them to contribute their unique skills and knowledge to the company's success.

Self-awareness: Successful leaders can confidently defend their acts, own their weaknesses, and argue for their views. Individually and collectively, they consider what they can do better in the future.

Transparency: Incredible leaders think about how their activities may affect others, modeling responsible behavior for their teams. They make requests for assistance when necessary and offer thoughtful criticism when prompted.

Trust: Trusting your team members and allowing them to use their initiative may improve morale and motivation. By including them in decision-making and giving them agency over their work, you demonstrate trust and enable them to do their best.

Ten Steps to Taking Responsibility as a Leader
You can learn to be a more responsible leader in many different ways. Though some leadership qualities are innate, many successful managers have developed, through deliberate exercise, the habit of holding themselves and their teams accountable. Taking the following steps can help you develop into a responsible leader at work:

Clarify goals
To develop into a responsible leader, it is essential first to clarify what has to be accomplished and how. Keeping all of a project's details in the open is beneficial.

Focus on the future
A leader's responsibility includes anticipating and preparing for the department's future. That shows them you take your duties seriously and gives them confidence in handling them. It also entails thinking about the future and owning up to one's history.

Gather feedback
Leaders who regularly solicit feedback from their teams can better hold themselves accountable for completing tasks and setting the stage for future success. Goals can be fine-tuned with feedback, and success can be determined.

Provide honest feedback
Encourage workers to take responsibility for their jobs by giving them frequent, constructive criticism. Insight into their development like this helps them improve their performance. Employees can learn to improve the quality of their work and accept responsibility for their actions by receiving and acting on constructive criticism.

Own up to your mistakes and achievements
When you can take ownership of your accomplishments and setbacks, you give your colleagues a more accurate picture of your work environment. To foster this, try replacing "I" with "we" in business-related conversations. This shows a high

level of responsibility to others, develops accountability, and fosters justice within the team.

Practice workload awareness

Increase your leadership accountability by learning to manage your workload better. Recognize your and your team's seasonal limitations, and take on what you can realistically do. It demonstrates that you know your limits and trust your coworkers to see the job through.

Ensure effective communication

It is your duty as a leader to facilitate several lines of communication and promote candid exchanges among staff members. You and your team members may benefit from holding one another accountable in this way.

Align objectives with the skillsets of the team

Assigning work to workers calls for in-depth familiarity with team abilities. Both can benefit from knowing each other's talents and weaknesses to fulfill their professional responsibilities. Implementing this strategy will help you reach your goals more quickly and show your staff that you value their expertise.

Host frequent meetings

Hold regular meetings to ensure everyone is pulling their weight. To assume responsibility for your actions and the team's success, you must be willing to explain requirements, discuss unfinished work, evaluate objectives, document progress, respond to queries, arrange performance checks, suggest new ideas, and accept feedback.

Encourage experimentation

Develop your abilities as a responsible leader through exploration and innovation. Teams learn to take ownership of the project's success or failure by pushing its boundaries.

The 7-Step Plan for Establishing Trust in Your Team

Having confidence in oneself and one's coworkers is crucial for achieving one's professional goals. You can learn how to establish trust and why it's vital by participating in trust-building events and assignments at work. Follow these seven suggestions to increase confidence among your team at work.

Foster communication

One of the best ways to create trust with your team is to encourage open lines of communication. Team members are more likely to stay informed and invested in a project if they regularly use a standardized communication channel.

Try to be transparent

Employee trust can be maintained through open communication, such as when team members share their worries about the project's progress or the timeline. A clear timeframe for the project can be more easily communicated in this way.

Talk to each member of the team separately

Having one-on-one conversations with every team member is a great way to build rapport and learn more about their professional and personal lives. Positive and trustworthy relationships at work can be fostered in this way.

Conduct team-building activities

Scavenger hunts, trust exercises, and sharing pyramids are just a few examples of games that can be used as team-building activities. They offer a way for people to meet one another in an informal yet trustworthy setting.

Encourage collaboration

Team members might feel more at ease and learn to work together effectively if encouraged to collaborate. Relation-ships can be strengthened while they work together or inde-pendently on activities.

Show your appreciation

Motivating team members to keep up their vital work requires gaining their trust and establishing solid working relationships.

Exhibit leadership qualities

Leading by example is the best way to earn the respect and admiration of your employees. It's crucial to demonstrate the kind of behavior and results you want from your team members. Train your staff by becoming an expert on a new piece of software.

Developing one's leadership skills should be an ongoing goal

The most striking aspect of this collection of work is its focus on leadership qualities, including decisiveness under pressure, language proficiency, collaborative skills, and an overarching perspective. Leaders should always continue learning since there are always new skills they may apply to their role. The benefits listed below are just the tip of the iceberg for leaders who continue their education throughout their careers.

Learn new perspectives

Leaders can gain insight into a topic by hearing other people's perspectives. It inspires people to examine issues and situations from several angles, which can reveal insights they hadn't previously considered.

The business world is constantly evolving

Leaders should keep up with the industry by reading books, listening to podcasts, and enrolling in online leadership courses because technology and markets are evolving rapidly. Leaders who keep up with industry developments are better equipped to make choices that will have a lasting influence on the firm.

Improve your current skills

Leaders must continuously develop themselves and look for new methods to hone their abilities. Keeping one's skill set current and valuable to the company should be a priority. The team's enhanced abilities are helpful to the company's growth, and everyone benefits when everyone on the team benefits.

Help create a more decisive leader

A leader's eagerness to learn is a commendable quality since it inspires followers to make similar investments in themselves. Leaders who prioritize learning can gain access to fresh knowledge, broaden their perspectives, and develop their analytical abilities. A company's bottom line might benefit from an employee's commitment to lifelong learning. The result may be an improved staff with a more incredible drive to produce excellent results.

It drives innovation

People who value education are more receptive to criticism and new ideas suitable for the company and its clientele. The adaptability of their unique abilities motivates them to keep learning new things. The greatest obstacle to innovation is people's reluctance to take risks due to the fear of societal judgment. Leaders who care about their teams' growth foster an environment where employees are comfortable taking risks, sharing ideas, and receiving feedback.

It builds great teams

Microsoft CEO Satya Nadella credits adopting a growth mindset for the company's recent success. The new 'Model Coach Care' management structure was recently established, and it calls for managers to demonstrate growth mindset behaviors themselves, coach colleagues, and provide opportunities for employee development. Nadella's leadership approach led to Microsoft's record-breaking success and current worth of $1 trillion.

It makes us resilient

Numerous studies have shown that adopting a growth mindset increases adaptability, initiative, creativity, and focus. Managers of crises should be confident in their ability to obtain and apply information and constantly on the lookout for new data sources. To steer their organizations toward success and ensure their continued survival and expansion, leaders who are devoted to lifelong learning will recognize the need for change and incentivize employees to try new things.

Creative Ideas for Showing Appreciation to Employees

Workers should be made aware of how much their efforts are valued. One way to express gratitude is with a gift card or other present. However, acknowledgment is more than just a nod of approval; it also requires honesty and originality. Here are 15 unique approaches to demonstrating gratitude to employees:

You can go right with food

Everyone enjoys a good meal now and then. You can use the money you've set aside for the break room to buy a gorgeous food arrangement to share with your coworkers. The office will benefit from improved communication and collaboration thanks to the food present. Employee morale will be boosted as a result.

Get Social

Using social media to spread positive news and celebrate staff's achievements is a great idea. A photo and brief description can showcase an employee's accomplishments or share information about them that their present coworkers might not already know.

Gamify Appreciation

Through corporate gamification, employees can be recognized for their efforts by claiming tasks and earning points based on the value of those tasks. A corporate rewards portal allows workers to cash in their points for prizes such as paid time off, flexible scheduling options, and educational grants.

Give the gift of fitness

Team well-being can be significantly improved with the use of a fitness incentive. Rewards for meeting fitness targets, complimentary gym memberships, or even an in-house fitness center are all viable options. You can boost your workforce's health, happiness, and productivity by incentivizing good behavior.

Throw a surprise party

A member of your team may close a huge deal. Or, introducing the new product line may go off without a hitch. When this occurs, it's cause for surprising jubilation. A surprise party can inspire workers who deserve recognition.

Splash some cash

Financial reward is only one of the most original incentives. However, only some employees will be satisfied with a monetary bonus. Cash gifts are a great way to show employees you appreciate their contributions to the company's success.

Move away from the desk

Employees regularly exceed expectations at work. They may put in more time at work, forego leisure activities, or forego sleep if it means getting the task done. Overachievers might be rewarded in these situations by being given extra free time. Let them go home and spend the rest of the day with their loved ones or engage in their favorite activities.

Take advantage of FaceTime

Acknowledgment is a very individual act. This should be tailored to the preferences of your team. A company's leadership must meet individually with each employee. Please take advantage of that moment to learn how they would like to be appreciated.

Give out vacation days

Showing employees you are thankful can be as simple as giving them a day off. Grant them time off that they can use as they like.

Invite them to the mall

The budget may only sometimes allow for regular bonus payments. However, you appreciate the concept of employee appreciation gifts but are concerned about draining company coffers too quickly. In that case, you can always give your employees occasional monetary awards. You may reward star employees with gift cards occasionally so they can take their families to the mall.

Boost their LinkedIn profile

Investing in an employee's future is a fantastic strategy to boost morale and productivity. There are additional ways to demonstrate respect for staff members. Creating a positive LinkedIn recommendation for a standout employee is a terrific way to do this. They can use advice like this to succeed in their current position.

Get Away Together

It's always appreciated when leadership acknowledges the efforts of the entire team. A company retreat could be something you do once a year. One way to show appreciation for your staff is to treat them to a Caribbean vacation or a company outing to a five-star hotel in the city.

Happy Birthday!

Celebrating someone else's birthday is usually well-received. However, it would help if you remember that some prefer to keep their birthdays a secret. Staff birthdays are best celebrated with a company-wide catered lunch and birthday cake unless the individual in question expressly declines.

Recognize your winners
Setting up a rewards and recognition system for staff is a smart move. A systematic program will make it easier to show appreciation to employees regularly. Team members can collaborate with you to develop touching ways to show appreciation to the employees.

Let them appreciate each other
Motivating employees requires only tiny, consistent displays of appreciation. Create a streamlined system for staff and management to express gratitude to one another. For instance, a technological platform could be used to implement a plan for simple praise delivery.

Employee Recognition Matters
Recognizing and rewarding employees is crucial to a successful business. Workers like it when management treats them like individuals and looks out for their best interests. Managers who want to create trust with their employees should demonstrate genuine appreciation at all stages of their stay. In the long run, employees who feel appreciated will be more willing to put in extra effort for the organization.

Going Beyond "Thank You"
The most prosperous companies are those whose workers are the happiest. Annual retreats and opportunities for employees to volunteer are just two examples of the kinds of activities that can help businesses demonstrate their appreciation. Still, there are plenty of other methods that can be used. Employee participation, output, retention, and morale can all benefit from such gatherings.

Keep your team satisfied and on task

Employees' desires and needs are considered, and the company's core values are reinforced, all of which favor bottom-line results. A successful employee recognition program can have a beneficial effect on the whole business.

Motivational Story

Growing up, my siblings and I experienced a modest upbringing that didn't offer many luxuries. This modesty translated into a rather basic education for us. However, amidst my years at the school, a shimmering dream took root in me—a dream of someday helming a prominent company within my nation. It was a distant aspiration, laden with yearning. I was under the impression that attaining such lofty positions necessitated an exorbitant investment in top-tier education, a prospect that seemed beyond reach during that phase of my life.

Over time, a new understanding began to take shape. I realized that the path to success wasn't solely paved by the absence of resources; rather, it was defined by one's inherent strengths. This was particularly evident in the realm of leadership. The abilities you possess, whether innate or honed over time, as well as your adeptness at human interaction, gradually mold and elevate your professional profile. It dawned on me that my journey to becoming a leader wasn't exclusively reliant on external factors but was closely linked to cultivating these inner capabilities.

Consider the tale of Pablo, a colleague I met during my initial foray into the corporate world. Like me, Pablo hadn't been endowed with privileges from the outset. His background didn't set him on a trajectory toward grand opportunities. Yet, he exhibited a rare talent for bringing people together and harnessing their collective strengths. He transformed challenges into collaborative endeavors, demonstrating that leadership could be a force cultivated from within.

* * *

CHAPTER 2
LISTENING AND COMMUNICATING WITH EMPATHY

One way to develop as a leader is to communicate better with others. The lines of communication between upper management and their employees can be constantly improved. The success of a business is directly proportional to the level of communication within its management team. Managers' ability to clear up confusion and manage problems in the workplace is greatly enhanced by the maintenance of open channels of communication. Workers will enjoy their jobs more and think highly of their supervisors. The success of every workplace depends on the manager's ability to keep lines of communication open with their staff. Effectively conveying your ideas to your team is crucial to your success as a manager or leader.

Improve your communication skills

To get our points across, words must be unambiguous and comprehensive. Acquiring the ability to communicate with candor, sympathy, and comprehension is essential. The best way to get better at speaking is to practice. If you want to step up your communication game in the workplace, try some of these suggestions.

Consider your audience

The success of your message delivery depends on your familiarity with your target audience. The recipient's age, gender, marital status, race, ethnicity, income, subject knowledge, level of education, and professional experience can all impact how they respond to your message. For example, if you're promoting a fast-food restaurant, you want your message in front of starving people.

Practice active listening

A vital component of any successful conversation is active listening. Strategies include using nonverbal cues, subtle words, open-ended queries, and reserving judgment. Think about who you're talking to before you say anything, and use active listening to get to the bottom of what they want.

Spell out your meaning as clearly as you can

You may have something to say when you've determined who you're talking to and their goals, objectives, and interests. The 5 C's of communication can help you accomplish this goal by ensuring that your message is:

- Clear
- Complete
- Concise
- Correct
- Compassionate

Think about how you can word your messages so they have as many qualities as possible.

Make effective use of the proper channel

Successful communication relies heavily on using the appropriate medium or platform. Be aware of who you're talking to, make sure your message is clear, and use a proper setting or medium. Thinking about who you're talking to, listening actively, being clear about what you're saying, and picking the correct medium are all ways to improve your communication skills.

Communication skills every manager needs

Leaders that need help to get their messages across will prioritize team building, motivation, trust, and swift change management. Getting other people to alter their behavior, collaborate, and develop more confidence is crucial. One way to grow as a leader is to improve communication skills.

Capacity to change how you say things

Problems like priority confusion and emotional overload are often the result of different communication methods. Knowing your leadership style will help you gauge how others see and respond to you in the workplace. Your ability to influence others and advance organizational objectives depends on your communication skills.

Transparency

Open communication can close the gap between executives, workers, and upper-level management. Leaders may establish trust and encourage people to contribute ideas and work together by being transparent about the company's objectives, opportunities, and obstacles. Recognizing that you made a mistake might help foster a more accepting environment where active problem-solving occurs.

Clarity

Share your clear expectations for the outcome of a project or strategic endeavor with your staff. If your message isn't getting through, try simplifying it or asking for more information or assistance. Employees will be less disoriented and more invested in the process.

Possession of open-ended question-asking skills

Asking employees open-ended questions is a great way to gain insight into their feelings, ideas, and aspirations. To avoid confusion, use the TED method:

- "Tell me more."
- "Explain what you mean."
- "Define that term or concept for me."

Using such terms while communicating with your team can help you get more detailed, well-considered responses and give you a better sense of what they need from you to succeed.

Empathy

A leader's capacity to put themselves in another person's shoes is crucial. Although 96% of respondents to a recent survey said employer empathy was important, 92% of those polled thought it was undervalued. Responding with compassion can strengthen relationships overall.

Open body language

Focusing on body language to get your point across is crucial because nonverbal clues are the most significant aspect of communication. Focus on the other person, make eye contact, and smile to show that you care.

Accepting criticism and adjusting the course

By asking for opinions, you can grow as a leader and gain the respect of your team. Consider the recommendations, be bold, and admit that you can't apply some immediately. You must demonstrate to your employees that you've heard them if you want them to believe you'll do something about their suggestions.

Strategies for Improving Leadership Listening Skills

It's common for leaders to advance through the ranks by asserting themselves as individuals. Still, once they're part of a leadership team, they must learn to listen as much as they talk. Active listening aims to make the other person feel heard and understood by paying close attention to what they are saying. It's easy to pick up the necessary skills, but becoming proficient will take some time.

- Pay attention to both the person speaking and the message. Give the person talking your undivided attention, and refrain from making snap judgments or planning your response until they've finished speaking. Please focus on the speaker's facial expressions and gestures as well as their words. Since most people have gotten used to tuning out their mental chatter, this can be the trickiest stage to master.
- Communicate your attention. Body language and gestures are powerful ways to show people you are engaged with what they are saying and not daydreaming. Active listening involves some behaviors, including maintaining eye contact with the speaker, sitting or standing in an open position, and smiling or nodding occasionally.
- Listen attentively and acknowledge the other person's thoughts. Using expressions like "Uh huh" or "I see" is appropriate to show that you understand. This reply demonstrates your attentiveness without implying your agreement with the other person. It's an excellent method for tuning out background noise and listening to what the other person is saying.
- Don't interrupt. This is another challenging phase since the brain naturally wants to provide a solution before the speaker has finished talking. Interrupting demonstrates a lack of tolerance and disrespect, especially if an argument is presented

instead of a question. Worse, it hinders both your comprehension and the speakers. Patience is a critical component of active listening, as is waiting for the speaker to finish each point before jumping in with questions.

- Build rapport. Interact with the speaker by asking questions or paraphrasing what you've heard after you've listened for a bit. Use phrases like "I'm not sure I understand" or "What I'm hearing you say is..." That indicates your attentiveness and opens many learning opportunities.
- Respond genuinely. As a listener, your goal should be to learn something new and gain insight or comprehension. Respond with openness and honesty while still maintaining appropriate decorum. Respond to the problem rather than the individual if there is a dispute or argument.

Practice transparent leadership

Managers need to work hard to gain their staff's trust and allegiance. That cannot be easy because the new manager's rank, authority, and network may still need to be discovered. Being transparent and honest about your managerial choices is essential. Open and ethical leadership is good for the company since it increases trust and efficiency in the work-place. Here is how you can become a transparent leader:

Set clear expectations

Create an open and honest work environment by communicating expectations to staff. Weekly team meetings, performance reviews, and one-on-one time should all be incorporated to communicate and share company develop-ments. Establish a standard for your team based on how you want to receive and distribute information.

Have an open dialogue about the future of your business

Team members can improve their existing positions and aim for higher positions if given accurate information about the company's condition and future. Sharing common objectives and initiatives outside formal meetings can also improve employee retention.

Locate the problems that have been affecting your business and address them openly

It is essential to give workers a safe space to express their frustrations and a sense of community during tough times. If problems within your company aren't addressed, it could create an atmosphere of mistrust and insecurity. You can only make progress as a leader if you can acknowledge failure.

Open up a channel for feedback

Leaders and managers should regularly evaluate each other's performance so that each can learn from the other's feedback. Also, talk to HR about providing anonymous feedback via tools or survey forms.

Honor your commitments

Transparent leadership involves sticking to your word, even when it means making unpopular choices. Think carefully about maintaining open communication with your team without exposing unnecessary details about yourself or others. Keep contacts focused on helping workers make informed choices in the future.

The Importance of Empathetic Communication at Work

To communicate with empathy, you must put yourself in the other person's shoes to comprehend what will make them feel most secure and loved by what you say. Being approachable and attentive to the other person is essential for resolving any issues. How to have a compassionate conversation

- Get back to clients as soon as possible. Whether it's a world crisis or a support ticket, it demonstrates that you care about people's feelings when you respond quickly to the situation without turning it into a marketing campaign.

- Draw motivation from your introspective listening. Restating someone else's feelings in their own words validates their experience and removes the need for interpretation. Furthermore, it aids the individual in feeling heard and understood by validating their emotional experience.
- Recognize the validity of other people's experiences, even if you disagree with them. Some customers may feel uneasy about your recent modifications to your terms and conditions. You can say to your clients that they can rest assured that we will always be transparent with you and give you the freedom to make informed decisions.
- Be accountable. No matter how well-intentioned a message may be, if it causes distress to its recipients, the company responsible for the notification must bear the consequences.
- Make appropriate use of emotional language when writing. Use a dynamic analysis tool to ensure you're not intentionally inciting negative feelings in your audience.

How to show more Empathetic Leadership

One who possesses empathy can identify with and share another person's emotional state or life story. The two emotions are commonly confused; however, there is a significant difference between compassion and empathy. The workplace greatly benefits from employees who can empathize with others. The following are actions that leaders can take to demonstrate empathy in the workplace and with their direct reports:

Keep an eye out for anyone showing indications of burnout

Burnout is a serious issue in today's workplaces, and stress and pressure only make it worse. Leaders with compassion recognize the warning signals of overworked staff and act proactively to alleviate their stress by, for example, doing more regular check-ins.

Be genuinely concerned about the well-being of others and their goals in life

One way to demonstrate empathy as a leader is to tailor assignments to the strengths and interests of individual team members. To increase productivity and morale, kindness in the office can go a long way.

Exhibit empathy and the desire to assist an employee in need

A leader with empathy understands that their team members are unique people who may require assistance at critical junctures. To create a comfortable environment where team members can feel secure speaking up when necessary, they maintain open lines of communication and promote openness.

Be sympathetic when others talk about suffering a loss

Managers need to connect with their staff personally; empathetic leadership is crucial in making that happen. We can all respond with empathy and support to a grieving teammate, even if we can't relate to the specific loss they are experiencing.

How to Improve Your Body Language as a Manager

Leadership body language should emphasize encouragement, sympathy, and connection with followers. Your body language may be the cause of your ineffective leadership style. Learn how to put your body language to good use with these pointers.

Eye Contact

The power of eye contact lies in its ability to convey assurance, strength, and trust. Observing the eye color of the people you speak with can help you make more meaningful eye contact. That way, you can keep eye contact while conversing.

Authentic Smiles

Always have a welcoming expression on your face. Due to the pressures and obligations of leadership, you may only feel like smiling sometimes. Leaders with an inflated sense of importance often overlook the value of humor and lightheartedness in the workplace. On the other hand, if you smile at someone genuinely, they may feel more comfortable and strike up a discussion with you.

Confident Posture

An insecure or confident stance can be conveyed through your body language. You give off an impression of insecurity if you cross your arms, slouch, or adopt a small stance. Having your arms outstretched, shoulders back, and legs straight gives off an air of authority. You'll come across as a strong leader worthy of respect and admiration if you adopt this stance.

Hand Gestures

Using your hands to express yourself shows you care about the other person and the conversation. You give off the idea that you don't care about the case if you stand there with your hands folded or clinched in front of you. People who work with their hands frequently are seen as more competent by those around them. Use expressive hand gestures when you speak to win over your listeners.

Pay attention to the clues you're receiving

You must pay attention to the words people use and their body language. Is the person you're talking to leaning back from you with their arms crossed in a defensive posture? This could make them nervous or hesitant to trust you. Make the appropriate gestures and facial expressions. Is their body language one of openness and interest? If that is the case, your efforts have been fruitful. One way to get your message across is to mimic the body language of those around you.

Relax

Tenseness is one issue that may arise from an emphasis on body language. Shoulders can rise, and stiffness can set in if one dwells too much on body language. Failing a confident demeanor is not easy, but it's worth the effort. You can improve the outcome of your communication by just taking a deep breath and smiling before you start talking.

Show Confidence

Last, but not least, remember to utilize confident body language. Keep your chin up and your shoulders back while standing and talking to someone. Keep your head up and stop reaching for your pockets. Take long, measured strides. You can use your hands, but if you touch your face or neck, it will appear nervous. Your success on the job depends on the confidence your team sees reflected in your body language.

Methods and Strategies for Effective Feedback Exchange

Being able to take criticism is a vital ability for every leader. It could significantly improve efficiency and morale in the workplace. Anyone working in a team should make it a regular part of their profession to provide and receive feedback. What happens depends on how you express this criticism. I have compiled a list of the top five considerations to make before giving feedback:

Use positive language

Use as many upbeat expressions as possible when providing criticism. When we feel threatened, our natural response is to defend ourselves. If you frame it favorably, the other person will be more receptive to what you say. You should also employ the right tone and delivery. The recipient's reaction to your criticism will depend on how you express yourself.

Please pay more attention to what is occurring than to who is causing it

When providing criticism, it's essential to zero in on the events rather than assign blame. When working in a team, strong teamwork skills are a necessity. Other people's actions may prevent you from reaching your objectives. Remember that the goal of constructive criticism is to help the recipient grow.

Be clear and specific

Being as detailed and specific as possible while providing feedback is essential. The purpose, methodology, and outcome must all be clearly articulated. The individual will be better able to concentrate on making the necessary adjustments.

Choose the appropriate time

The most critical points are the emphasis on providing timely feedback and directly addressing the undesirable behavior or activity. When giving criticism, it's best to do so one-on-one rather than in a group environment like a meeting or presentation. Feedback should be used to improve working conditions, not as an opportunity to embarrass others. In the business world, sensitivity goes a long way.

Recognize a job done well

There are other ways to provide comments than by pointing out mistakes. Someone who has gone above and beyond their duties should be told directly. By publicly recognizing and rewarding the efforts of those who have gone above and beyond, you may boost morale on the job and encourage further success.

Considerations When Receiving Feedback
Be open to feedback

Pay attention and ask clarifying questions while receiving feedback from a coworker or supervisor. Constructing a survey with free-form questions is an effective way to solicit customer feedback. The next set of clients will have a more pleasant time thanks to the insights gleaned from the survey and implemented on the job.

Watch your nonverbal communication

When receiving criticism, you may tense up and turn away from your coworker. The expressions on your face also reveal your state of mind. Being responsive entails keeping an open mind, not getting defensive, and not harboring any ill will toward the individual providing criticism.

Evaluate the comments and take action

Consider the comments now that you have them. Think about how you might change your behavior in light of the advice and new understanding you've gained to boost your productivity at work.

Ask for help if needed

Even after receiving feedback, we may need guidance on what to do next or how to implement it. Be bold about asking for assistance from a coworker or even a supervisor if you need it. Check-in and get more input to determine if your adjustments were successful.

Feedback from subordinates and superiors is essential for leaders who want to improve their skills

First and foremost, an excellent leader's responsibility is to foster a culture where employees feel safe providing and receiving feedback. Employees who can take criticism and use it to better themselves are invaluable. If you care about the team's growth, output, and banter, you'll try to comprehend what they say. The best way to handle team recommendations is as follows:

- Be humble. Put aside your pride and listen to your staff without making any judgments. Don't make it about them if it's unsolicited. Think of it as a chance for you and your company to learn and improve, regardless of the outcome.
- Listen to understand. Keep an open mind, pay attention, and ask follow-up questions as you listen. Don't pretend or dismiss what they're saying; instead, listen with the intent of learning. You should seek clarity before applying your leadership perspective to what they tell you. Don't zone out; instead, listen intently to learn.
- Stay calm. You're being defensive if you're upset by what someone else is saying but refuse to own up to your mistakes. It can make you overreact by rolling your eyes, blaming the victim, or even justifying bad behavior. Avoiding this situation requires an honest attempt to grasp the employee's point of view and remember that they are only trying to assist.
- Trust them and assume the best. Give the person who gives you feedback the benefit of the doubt; they may be trying to tell you something important for you to know. Treat the critic with love and respect even if the critique is harsh.
- Show your appreciation. You can learn a lot from some constructive criticism. Any other comments will be completely off-base. In any case, reflect on the information your employee provided and express your gratitude to them for having the courage to open up to you. You may need to

rethink the wording of a policy if employees need to correct it consistently.

- Respond thoughtfully. Thank an employee for providing input, take some time to consider how best to address their concerns, and then respond. Even if you disagree, this will show your team you care about them as leaders.

Motivational Stories
Financial Failure to Fortune

A few years ago, Kimra Luna supported her young family on food stamps and other government aid. Even though she had trouble making ends meet, Kimra never gave up on her goal of starting her own profitable business. She had moderate success with her enterprises, but more was needed to provide for her family and independence. These attempts, however, inspired her to pursue an education in digital marketing. She quickly became proficient in live blogging, social media branding, and Facebook advertisements.

Luna started holding webinars where she taught business owners about marketing. She immediately began mentoring company owners who sought her expertise in marketing. She eventually stopped caring about everything but hosting and attending online marketing webinars. Yahoo! Finance reports that in the first week of selling her online marketing webinars in the middle of 2014, she made $10,000. She had made almost $160,000 by the end of the year. The current annual sales for Luna's team are $750,000.

From Sleeping in a Parked Car to Having Three Private Jets of Your Own
John Paul DeJoria, co-founder of Paul Mitchell

John Paul DeJoria once operated his business out of the back of his car. A first-generation American, "DeJoria was born in Los Angeles," according to his Entrepreneur bio. Before he reached 10, he was already a successful businessman, selling greeting cards and newspapers door-to-door. He even joined a gang. Later, he borrowed $700 to start his company.

How One Company Grew from Paying the Minimum Wage to a Billion Dollars

Mark Cuban became a household name after his appearance on "Shark Tank," but he didn't always enjoy financial success. Cuban started as a struggling entrepreneur selling garbage bags door-to-door.

"It's only necessary to be right once, no matter how many times you've tried and failed."

"Mark Cuban"

From then on, he worked various odd jobs to make ends meet. He made his first million when he launched a computer consulting business. At that point, he saw an opportunity to establish a web broadcasting empire that would earn him a billion dollars. He took over as majority owner of the NBA's Dallas Mavericks in 2000, leading the team to championship success.

* * *

CHAPTER 3
EMBRACE EMOTIONAL INTELLIGENCE AND SELF-AWARENESS

How Self-awareness in leadership can make you a better manager

WHY KNOWING YOURSELF WILL MAKE YOU A BETTER LEADER

Understanding oneself entails keeping tabs on one's feelings, reactions, strengths, flaws, triggers, and motivators. Leaders can learn to better respond to different events and individuals, allowing them to avoid conflict and serve as an example to their teams. The first step in developing into a better leader is realizing your shortcomings and working to address them. It can be complicated, but self-awareness can make you a better leader. For more introspection, consider these suggestions:

- Keep an open mind. Keeping your emotions in check will make starting conversations with new people more accessible. A good leader is attentive to their employees and takes their feedback seriously. That demonstrates you are not a self-centered perfectionist but a valuable team member. If you open up your business to input and ideas from others, you'll find more creative ways to solve problems.

- Know your strengths and weaknesses. Those with a solid grasp of themselves know their strengths and weaknesses.
- Stay focused. Making connections is essential for leadership, but it takes work while your mind is elsewhere. Training your capacity to focus for long periods without distractions, such as your phone, email, or social media, can significantly increase your productivity.
- Set boundaries. It is the responsibility of the leader to impose order. Keep a good disposition, but discover how to say "no" when the time comes effectively. Protect the worth of your work and efforts by taking them seriously and delineating strict limits for yourself.
- Learn to identify your emotional triggers. People in tune with themselves are aware of their emotions as they arise. Do not ignore or try to stifle your feelings; learn to deal with them. Don't rush to express your feelings; give yourself time to process them first.
- Embrace your intuition. People who consistently achieve their goals develop the ability to trust their gut when making important decisions and are willing to take calculated risks. Competition and survival are the guiding principles of your natural inclinations. Trust your instincts; they will guide your future steps.

- Practice self-discipline. Influential leaders often have the trait of being highly disciplined individuals. They possess the undivided attention that is necessary for successful leadership.
- Consider the results of your actions. Sometimes, we behave hastily without considering the repercussions. An integral part of growing self-awareness is realizing your feelings and how your reactions to those feelings impact others around you. The more you respect others, the more they will respect you.
- Apologize when necessary. One of the hallmarks of mature self-awareness is the realization that not all mistakes require an apology. Maybe you've been distant or angry with your staff as of late. Accepting responsibility, offering a heartfelt apology, and committing to a new course of action is the best way to resolve a situation.
- Ask for feedback. Self-aware people know themselves well enough to know what they need to know, but it takes courage (and self-awareness) to ask for an honest employee review. Doing so can help you overcome your bias toward yourself (a tendency we all have) and gain a more objective perspective.

What is Emotional Intelligence?

"Emotional intelligence" (EI) is a person's ability to be in tune with themselves and maintain composure in social settings. Forging and maintaining meaningful personal and professional relationships is vital. Understanding the significance of emotions and learning to recognize and manage them is crucial. A leader's ability to maintain composure and keep moving forward in the face of adversity is directly related to their EI.

It's Crucial to Have Emotional Intelligence to be an Effective Leader

Understanding employees' emotions and motivations is essential for executives in assessing their performance, and this is where emotional intelligence comes in. This strategy encourages leadership development, innovation, and originality beyond efficiency, timeliness, productivity, and target. Effective leaders have a deep understanding of emotional intelligence. Below, I've outlined the elements of emotional intelligence that contribute to effective leadership:

Self-awareness

Recognizing one's talents and shortcomings, controlling one's emotions and how they affect others, and cultivating humility as a leader are all aspects of self-awareness. How, then, can you grow your self-awareness?

- **Keep a journal.** Keeping a journal can increase your insight into who you are. Spending as little as a few minutes daily writing down your thoughts can help you develop a higher level of self-awareness.
- **Slow down.** Stop and think about what's causing your anger or whatever intense feeling you're having. Always keep in mind that you have the power to decide how you will respond.

Self-regulation

Influential leaders focus on self-regulation and personal accountability, avoiding verbal attacks, emotional decisions, stereotyping, and compromising values. How, therefore, can you develop your capacity for self-control?

- **Know your values.** Consider your priorities and beliefs (or what you can call your "code of ethics") to make morally or ethically sound judgments on the spot.
- **Hold yourself accountable.** Stop passing the buck and start taking responsibility; that's the only way to gain respect and move forward.
- **Practice being calm.** Be conscious of your behavior and refrain from yelling at others when faced with a difficult situation. You can calm yourself by using deep breathing techniques and writing down your negative thoughts. That serves to test your reactions and maintain justice.

Motivation

Self-motivated leaders are steadfast in their pursuit of excellence and never settle for mediocrity. What can you do to boost your enthusiasm?

- Ask yourself why you're working so hard. Consider why you're unhappy in your current position. New and inspiring mission statements are critical for problem resolution and fostering a productive work atmosphere.
- Know your position: Analyze what drives you to be a leader and where you could use some help to become more effective.
- Despite setbacks and difficulties, maintain hope and look for the bright side. Adopt this frame of mind by looking for the bright side of every experience, whether meeting a new person or remembering a lesson from years ago.

Empathy

All essential leadership skills are the ability to put oneself in another person's shoes, cultivate team members, fight unfairness, provide constructive comments, and listen to people in need. How do you work on your capacity for empathy?

- Think like the other person. It's simple to argue in favor of your own beliefs. Indeed, it is yours by right! But try to put yourself in the shoes of those involved.
- Observe nonverbal cues. Body language can convey negative messages, such as biting the lips and crossing the arms and feet. Being able to interpret body language can help leaders respond appropriately and get to the bottom of people's genuine emotions.
- Respond to feelings. Your assistant will work late again if you ask him to. Confront his feelings head-on by letting him know you appreciate his hard work and understand his displeasure. One solution is to have everyone take Monday off to help cut down on late nights.

Social Skills

Excellent communication, adaptability to new situations, and tactful problem-solving are hallmarks of leaders with great social skills. By leading by example and encouraging their team, they are experts at navigating change and serving as role models. Exactly how, therefore, can one acquire sociability?

- Learn about conflict resolution. A leader's ability to mediate disputes between employees, clients, or suppliers is crucial. If you want to be successful, you need to learn how to deal with conflicts.

- Learn how to express yourself better. How effective is your verbal exchange?
- Master the art of giving compliments to others. Leaders who are generous with their praise might win the devotion of their teams. Mastering the art of effusive praise is challenging but rewarding work.

How leaders can safeguard their own and their teams' emotional well-being

Leaders in today's fast-paced and unpredictable businesses have challenges in crisis management, stress management, and keeping tabs on employees' mental health. Adaptability and self-interest are essential qualities for leaders. Given the confusion, workers need to brace themselves for challenges mentally. Here are some suggestions for fostering the mental health of your workforce.

FOR LEADERS TO PROTECT THEMSELVES:

Let go of your high hopes

You should give yourself a break for the time being. To prioritize your health, it may be helpful if you cut back on some of your obligations. Take care of yourself by allowing yourself to delegate responsibilities while meeting your critical deadlines and deliverables.

Stay connected

It can be challenging to assist all of your team members during commotion. It would be best if you did not try to perform this on your own and will need assistance. Share your difficulties with someone you trust or some close coworkers. One option for dealing with problems and finding answers is to form "reciprocity circles" with friends and class-mates. Seek the advice of an expert if necessary.

Compartmentalize your "worry time"

It would help if you prepared for the worst-case scenario as well as the most likely one. Reserve a whole day for this endeavor and focus on the end goal. Prepare for the worst, but be ready to act if required.

LEADERS' ROLE IN FOSTERING TEAM MEMBERS' SUCCESS

Learn about the programs and services your company provides for mental health

Find out what the company offers in the way of help for workers who are struggling with their mental health. Give them a detailed guide on registering for the required certi-fication.

Show them how it's done by taking care of your mental health

Reduce the taboo surrounding mental health by discussing what you're doing to stay well. Promoting an excellent work-life balance and showing that you value your mental well-being may inspire your team to do the same.

Keep the lines of communication open at all times

The well-being of the team and its ability to triumph over adversity depend on an open line of communication between its members. Regular check-ins, huddles, and online open offices should be considered. Refrain from bombarding them with messages and appointments. Talk things through care-fully. Schedule a "no meeting day" every so often to get ahead.

If necessary, readjust your expectations

Employees can feel less pressure when their duties and the expected output are reviewed regularly. Instead of focusing on resilience training, try cutting down on unnecessary tasks and eliminating redundancies. Employees will be better able to handle their workload as a result. Help workers understand the value they provide to the company.

Reduced anxiety is a side effect of having well-defined, heartfelt goals. Learn what drives employees, have open discussions about their professional aspirations, and give them learning opportunities to help them succeed. By easing the way, you can improve workers' outlooks, sense of self-worth, and emotional well-being.

Emotional mastery is a hallmark of great leaders

Leadership requires emotional regulation since followers model their conduct after their leaders in times of stress. Leaders who can control their emotions are more likely to earn the respect and trust of their teams and act in the company's best interests. Controlling one's emotions entails remaining level-headed in the face of pressure, uncertainty, and conflict, actively selecting positive feelings, and avoiding their negative counterparts. Emotional regulation is linked to long-term happiness and is a trainable skill. Consider the following questions as a means of gauging your degree of emotional maturity:

- How will my words affect my staff before responding?
- Can I accomplish my goals by displaying my feelings here?
- Am I able to handle pressure if it arises suddenly?
- Before reacting, do I think about what I will say or do?
- In what ways can I control my feelings?
- Regarding long-term emotional regulation, am I using techniques like mindful meditation?

Here are some ways to gain more self-control over your emotions:

- Take your time. Leaders should take a moment to step back, gather their thoughts, and act. The capacity to control one's feelings, consider the outcomes of one's actions, and respond appropriately has increased. Leaders must be able to step back and view a problem from several angles to develop viable solutions.
- Be proactive. Leaders need emotional regulation and control skills to keep their mental health in check. Leaders can deal with their emotions and improve the situation by talking to their employees or taking a break from demanding responsibilities. The best leadership style is the best for the leader, the group, and the problem at hand.
- Engage in mindfulness practice. Leaders who practice mindfulness can better keep their emotions in check at work because they are more in tune with themselves and their surroundings. Acceptance, deep breathing exercises, and nonjudgmental thinking have all improved emotional regulation and well-being.

IN A CRISIS, THERE ARE THREE WAYS A LEADER CAN KEEP COOL

Successful leadership relies on fundamental skills like the capacity to motivate and guide individuals and the aptitude to assume control when required. As a result of the effects of stress on work performance and morale, these qualities become especially important in challenging times. When managers become overwhelmed, their teams become overwhelmed, leading to missed deadlines, blunders, and even the loss of customers. You might use three methods to lead your team through a crisis calmly.

Wait to Act

A leader takes stock of the situation and responds with composure and a strategy. Take a moment to collect your thoughts before replying in tense situations. That allows you to organize your thoughts and evaluate the situation objectively. Keeping calm and collected in difficult situations is crucial. Taking a breather before deciding can help you make the best possible one.

Build a Strong Support system

A leader's board of advisors can help them keep their feet on the ground and rally around their vision. Ensure the people you hire have high moral standards, a wide range of relevant experiences, and a high level of emotional intelligence. Maintain composure and make educated decisions by recruiting trustworthy management. The team's efforts, perspectives, and inquiries are crucial to the project's success. Therefore, it's essential to establish a solid foundation of support.

Understand the Reality of the situation

In times of crisis, it's important to keep things in perspective and recognize your limitations. Do what needs to be done from your most potent, composed self rather than reacting emotionally. Methodically approach problems, consult experts, establish priorities, and delegate responsibly. Keep going with the strategy you've made, counting on yourself and your group to get you through this.

BECOMING AN EFFECTIVE LEADER

You can only expect to rise to the top of the leadership ranks by doing regular work, keeping calm under pressure, showing flexibility in the face of change, and developing your brand of leadership. The advantages of leadership education go far beyond the business world. Participants in strategic leadership courses can assess their current skill levels, learn new techniques, and receive constructive criticism from instructors. Leaders at any stage of their careers can benefit from the multifaceted expertise of specialists, innovators, network builders, and futurists.

What role does mindfulness play in effective leadership?
While many leaders struggle to meet their commitments, they can benefit from taking a few minutes each day to practice mindfulness and reduce stress. That can boost efficiency for them and their subordinates. Being in the here and now and realizing the value of pausing to refocus is essential to cultivating mindful leadership.

The 5 Cs: characteristics of a mindful leader
The following are commonalities among those who lead with mindfulness:

Composure
Confronted with adversity, mindful leaders keep their cool and bring inner strength and optimism.

Compassion
Thoughtful leader accepts and appreciates themselves and others for who they are and their flaws. They are kind and sympathetic, always looking for the best in others and pushing them to develop to their most significant potential.

Connectivity
A conscientious leader appreciates the importance of every team member and how they all work together to achieve goals.

Curiosity
A nonjudgmental mindfulness leader looks for common ground and avoids making snap judgments. They pose thought-provoking questions, offer fresh viewpoints, and

encourage team members to contribute their ideas and insights.

Caliber

Effective leadership requires tapping into one's resources of strength and self-awareness. They are dedicated to doing an excellent job and achieve this by maintaining a relaxed and confident atmosphere inside the team.

How do you lead with mindfulness?

To keep their leadership style fresh and compelling, mindful leaders must tend to it often. There may be pushback against this method, but finding that happy medium between being and doing is crucial. The effectiveness of one's actions can be increased through deliberate self-development. Pick easy exercises that pique your attention to strengthen your mindful leadership abilities over time. Keep in mind that the trick is to construct them gradually and steadily.

Practice 1: Observe yourself.

Raise your introspection, openness, and empathy to help you develop. Take a Harvard Business Review mindfulness test to gauge your mental health and identify areas for improvement. Spend just two minutes a day on it for a week.

Practice 2: Breathe, leader, breathe.

Improve your physical and mental health by taking five deep breaths before every call or meeting. Don't just think about breathing; let it fill you up. This easy technique can improve focus and concentration in group settings. Put a Post-it note on your computer screen so you can see it every time you log in.

Practice 3: Wake up your senses.

Spend two minutes daily tuning in to your surroundings through any combination of sight, smell, taste, touch, or hearing. That allows you to disconnect from your thoughts and enjoy the moment.

Practice 4: Bring mindfulness to a meeting.
Pick one daily gathering where you will focus all your attention, senses, and energy on thoroughly engaging with and comprehending everyone there. You should analyze their enthusiasm, facial expressions, and body language in the first three to five minutes. Show genuine interest in what they say and try to see things from their perspective. Mastering mindfulness in just five minutes will give you the foundation to bring your entire self to the rest of the meeting. It can be done once, twice a week, or every week.

Are You Aware of Your Biases?

Leading a team of people is a massive obligation. When dealing with the sensitive issue of unconscious prejudice, you must be conscious of your team's behavior and your own. You may not even know the mental processes subconsciously influencing your actions and leadership style. As a result, you must recognize how your mental routines may be sabotaging your managerial efforts. In my quest to become a more welcoming leader, I have found the following methods to be particularly useful:
Recognize your personal biases. Then, learn how to improve your performance.
Recognize the existence of your unconscious prejudices and actively attempt to overcome them through self-study and introspection. Assumptions can be exposed, and people can be seen for who they are. If you want to make a difference as a leader, you need to take the time to question yourself. Other questions to ponder are as follows:

- "What do I believe?" How may these assumptions help or hinder myself and my coworkers?

- How do I handle meeting new individuals who come from different cultures? Do I subscribe to any preconceived notions about a specific demographic?
- As a manager, do I value and use my team's diversity?
- How would my coworkers describe my management approach if they were to tell others about working with me?
- Is there congruence between my words and deeds?
- "Can I empathize with the other person's situation, even if I can't relate?"

Paying close attention to your responses will reveal thought patterns illuminating additional prejudices you might harbor.

Let others challenge your assumptions

Both conscious and unconscious factors, such as prejudices developed early in life, influence one's sense of self. Engage in talks regarding microaggressions and harmful behaviors, and approach problems with an open mind and constructive intent. The following are conversation starters to use if someone calls your attention to your microaggressions or harmful actions.

- I value your honesty and openness in telling me that. What else have you seen that I ought to know about?
- I had seen it from that angle when you explained it to me. Please elaborate.
- We appreciate it. I had no idea. Knowing that we all have unconscious prejudices motivates me to work on developing my leadership skills. Please tell me anything additional regarding the results of my actions.

You will get more comfortable asking others for input, and they may be the ones to spark the realization that you have biases that need to be addressed.

Be open to feedback

To develop self-awareness, leaders must regularly assess their performance, solicit the opinions of a wide range of colleagues, and put that information to good use. It might be helpful to have guidance from mentors or dependable coworkers when pinpointing areas for improvement and putting plans into action. Share your projects and seek support for recommitment when you falter. That will help you stay on track.

Embrace diverse perspectives

Spending time with people from all walks of life might broaden your perspective and spark your imagination. Employee Resource Groups (ERGs) and LinkedIn community groups are great places to meet like-minded people and build professional ties. Choose your leaders, peers, and coworkers with care, and be open to and appreciative of their differences.

Learn new things by taking in a wide range of content, from books to podcasts to online communities. Make time to reflect on your leadership path and develop your sense of self to handle better the inevitable challenges you'll face.

Motivational Story
Navigating Stormy Seas: Leadership Under Pressure

A vivid memory comes to mind, one that encapsulates the challenge of handling intense situations with finesse. The tale revolves around Eli, a customer whose frustration sparked a tumultuous encounter with our operations manager, Charlie. Picture this: a regular day at the office, the hum of meetings and tasks in progress, when the atmosphere suddenly changed. Eli stormed in, her displeasure palpable, like a tempest clouding the room. The root cause? Unmet delivery commitments that had left her seething with frustration.

In this pivotal moment, Charlie stood as a beacon of steadfastness amidst the chaos. Amid a crucial meeting with his team, Eli's intrusion could have easily derailed focus and triggered an impulsive reaction. However, Charlie's years of honing emotional intelligence paid off. Instead of clashing with the irate customer, he chose a path of patience and poise. As Eli's words filled the air with tension, Charlie listened, absorbing her grievances without interruption. His restraint created a space for her pent-up emotions to find an outlet. Such composure was a testament to the power of self-control, a trait Charlie had meticulously cultivated over the years.

Once Eli's outburst subsided, Charlie's response was unexpected yet brilliantly strategic. Recognizing the value in addressing her concerns constructively, he extended an invitation for a conversation over coffee. The ensuing dialogue proved transformative, yielding more efficient agreements and a newfound understanding.

The impact of this incident rippled through the office, imparting a profound lesson on leadership in the face of adversity. Colleagues marveled at Charlie's composure, noting that in the face of relentless provocation, his restraint had set an example that transcended the bounds of professionalism. The encounter stood as a stark reminder that leadership isn't just about overseeing operations but about navigating complex interpersonal dynamics.

Reflecting on this narrative, it's evident that leadership isn't confined to boardrooms and strategies. The true test of leadership often arises from unexpected sources, beckoning us to demonstrate grace under fire. In the grand tapestry of management, every thread—no matter how unruly—contributes to the fabric of effective leadership.

* * *

I would love to hear from you!

Your support and review are vital in getting my book to fellow leaders. Please take a moment to leave an Amazon review – it only takes 60 seconds. Scan the QR code below or use the link in your Amazon order if you're outside the listed countries. Here's a quick guide:

Open your mobile camera.
Scan the QR code.
Share your thoughts and rating.

Your feedback means a lot.

Thank you!

CHAPTER 4
ARTICULATING WITH CLEAR COMMUNICATION AND EXPECTATIONS

Strategies for Managing Expectations that Great Leaders Use

Successful people and teams know how important it is to set and manage expectations. Unmet expectations result in frustration, poor performance, and missed deadlines. Leaders must set and convey these expectations effectively to ensure follower accountability and facilitate achieving set goals. If workers are falling short of your requirements, it may be time to reevaluate your methods of expectation setting, communication, and providing relevant context and timescales.

It's good business practice to make one's expectations crystal clear

So, why are clear expectations and management so important?

- Happier workers are the result of clear expectations. Employees feel more positive and comfortable knowing what is expected of them.

They approach work boldly, are confident in their talents, and attain goals without uncertainty.

- Clear expectations boost performance. When they understand expectations, employees are more likely to optimize efforts and focus on tasks that provide desired results.
- Clear expectations align priorities. Employees with understanding expectations comprehend the "why" behind their task, ensuring proper assignment sequence and motivation.
- The organization's objectives can be better understood when everyone knows what is expected of them. Clear expectations help employees grasp the organization's aims and connect everyday duties with its larger objectives, making achieving them more straightforward.
- Clear expectations increase teamwork. Explicit knowledge of expectations in the office creates alignment, ensuring everyone feels on the same page and contributes to the team's success.

Communication Is Critical!

Expectation setting and management are crucial parts of good communication, and leaders who need help communicating usually need more satisfaction with their staff's performance. To increase communication, leaders should practice constant awareness and be conscious of their abilities to interact effectively with others. Some leaders think individuals know what is expected, leading to irritation, communication breakdowns, and a more significant divide between staff and management.

Effectively Managing Expectations: A Trait of Great Leaders

Creating unambiguous expectations may still be challenging, even if you're actively working on your communication and articulation abilities. The great news is that I have some fantastic suggestions for you based on the practices of today's most influential leaders.

Assure Workers that They Can Ask Questions About Their Work.

Leaders often express expectations in one direction, leading to frustration and discontent. Leaders should clearly understand expectations, empower people to ask questions, and collaborate on common expectations to manage expectations effectively. Empowering people to question leaders increases the likelihood of attaining goals. Leading with vulnerability and encouraging people to ask questions leads to a more effective and successful communication process.

Don't Leave Expectations unspoken.

Leaders sometimes assume their employees can read their minds, leading to frustration and lower company productivity. It's vital to convey expectations clearly, even if they're apparent. Your perspective impacts your comprehension of expectations, so disclosing and explaining your position is crucial to ensuring you understand what you're asking.

Setting expectations begins on day one and continues indefinitely.

Establish expectations for employees before recruiting by offering job descriptions with critical functions, requirements, credentials, and skills. Communicate these expectations throughout interviews, orientation, and subsequent one-on-ones, ensuring open dialogue inside the organization.

The Power of Storytelling in Leadership Communications

One of the most influential forms of communication, storytelling fosters community and cultural identity. Many of us in the public relations field are tasked with developing the strategies, plans, and programs that contribute to establishing a positive and productive corporate culture. But how can we find narratives to share with our staff and clients that will truly resonate? Getting a handle on the story's backstory and essential elements is an excellent place to start.

Storytelling within organizations

Staff members can use stories to make these associations. Here are some pointers to help the higher-ups in your company make good use of storytelling:

- **Know the audience:** Determine the people your business interacts with and work to serve them better.
- **Maximize data:** Use the information you collect to your advantage, whether from an internal climate survey, a customer review, a complaint review, or any other source.
- **Be authentic:** Use the words of the leaders to tell the tale.
- **Tell people why or how:** Share your company's guiding principles and the reasoning behind them.
- **Humanize the story:** It's helpful to talk about common difficulties and setbacks to build trust and rapport.

Why Goal Setting Is Important For Leaders

Mastering goal-setting is essential for success as a solo entrepreneur, manager, or leader. Great leaders like Elon Musk, Steve Jobs, and Bill Gates excel at translating their visions into daily work, showcasing their mastery of goal-setting. The reasons why good leaders establish objectives are:

- Leaders who set goals are likelier to keep performing at a high level.
- Setting goals motivates workers to do their best.

Given the prevalence of untested, out-of-date assumptions about goal setting, it's worthwhile to analyze the topic using the experiences of successful business executives and organizations worldwide.

To keep performing at a high level, leaders need goals

Constant labor, the risk of burnout, and balancing personal and professional obligations are just a few of the difficulties associated with significant duties. When starting, people must figure out how to be their chief procurement, marketing, financial, and operating officers.

Leaders with sharp minds are likelier to see their projects through to completion

Leaders who set SMART objectives have a broader perspective. When making a choice, most people think about how it will influence their lives now and in the future. Leaders might benefit from stepping outside of their comfort zones to get clarity. With these objectives in mind, they will be able to lead effectively. Our daily plans would be based on those objectives.

Eisenhower Matrix

To put these into action, a leader must

The 34th President of the United States popularized the Eisenhower Matrix, a simple and effective tool for setting priorities and achieving one's objectives.

	Urgent	Not Urgent
Important	DO Do it Now.	DECIDE Schedule a time to do it.
Not Important	DELEGATE Who can do it for you?	DELETE Eliminate it.

The Eisenhower Matrix

In this step, you'll prioritize your objectives and determine your next action.

- Urgent and important: It's critical that you act right now.
- Important but not immediately pressing: Planning and knowing the right time are essential.
- Urgent but not important: Who can you entrust to handle this responsibility?
- Not urgent and not important: Ignore it.

They find endless motivation in the actions of a great leader

Leaders who can't get their teams to work together toward a common purpose will be limited in their accomplishments. CEO participation and motivation may improve if lofty goals are consistent with the company's overall strategy. The best leaders inspire their teams to work tirelessly, take calculated risks, and sacrifice personal gain for the company's greater good. Planning for the future is an endless cycle. Leaders who want to maintain their strength and fortitude must do what interests them and keep their heads down when things don't go as planned.

A leader should put these into practice by doing de following:

- Identify the overarching objective that you value the most.
- Daily self-reminders of your mission are essential.
- If you want to succeed despite setbacks, you must regularly adjust your approach.

Goal-setting is a powerful motivator for employees

The relevance of goal-setting extends beyond the success of an individual leader to the success of the business as a whole.

Employees are more productive and innovative when they have a goal to strive toward

Forward-thinking businesses are increasingly adopting goal-setting as an alternative strategy since it gives employees more autonomy in determining their objectives and developing plans for achieving them. Half of Google's new products are created during this 20% goal-setting phase, and the company benefits from the increased productivity.

A leader should put these into practice:

- Recognize that stress harms your ability to think creatively and solve problems.
- Inspire your staff by letting them choose their objectives.

A generation's morale might be boosted by setting lofty goals

Just as the reasons mentioned earlier provide leaders with unyielding motivation, so too do ambitious and enticing goals give the entire nation or corporation a sense of purpose to work through problems.

How do you incorporate slideshows or other visual aids into team meetings?

Team meetings are essential for facilitating cooperation, information sharing, and resolving issues, yet poorly organized gatherings can be tedious, disorienting, or counterproductive. Visual aids are a great way to improve team meetings in four key areas: planning, preparation, presentation, and follow-up.

Consider the meeting's goals, target demographic, attendees' prior experience and expertise, and how much time you have to select visual aids. Sticky notes for ideas, whiteboards for comments, and internet collaboration tools for data sharing and comments can all be worthwhile.

Visual aids and tools should be carefully planned and practiced to ensure they are clear, simple, relevant, and clutter-free. Maintain cohesion in color, typeface, picture, and motion. Make sure there are no hiccups on the technical end, and practice with a script or notes to quickly move from one thing to the next.

Confidently use visual aids in team meetings to bolster spoken discourse, highlight salient points, pique listeners' interest, and pave the way for more address, collaboration, or action. Make appropriate use of words, gestures, and eye contact to interact.

After a team meeting:

1. Ask participants what they thought of any slides or other visual aids that were used.
2. Send a summary, express gratitude, and request input for enhancements.
3. Evaluate progress, pinpoint problem areas, and bring your newfound knowledge to the next meeting.

What Makes a Great Story? Leadership Lessons through Storytelling

The business world is shifting swiftly, with increasingly complicated hierarchies and an overwhelming volume of data. Leaders in this setting need the persuasive power of stories to succeed. Employees are more motivated, investors and communities are aligned, and customers are engaged when businesses use storytelling. It's a low-cost method of generating value for businesses because engaging narratives are memorable, thought-provoking, and valuable for retaining information.

What makes storytelling so useful for leaders?

Storytellers have an advantage in attracting and retaining top talent, interacting with the media, securing funding, and forming strategic alliances. Both informally and formally, telling a story helps the listener connect with the speaker and retain more of the information being conveyed.

Among the many advantages of storytelling are the following:

- Draws attention to the kinds of teamwork you want to see more of.
- It facilitates long-term retention of complex knowledge
- It creates a profound connection with your readers.
- It enables you to impart the leadership lessons and principles that have guided your success.
- It encourages others to join your cause and works to change their minds.
- Motivates people to take action

How have well-known companies mastered the art of storytelling?

How do you define a successful brand? How do you define an excellent leader? Studying the branding and customer communication strategies of the world's most successful organizations can teach you valuable lessons about the art of storytelling.

Airbnb example

Airbnb's advertising strategy centers on the human-interest stories of the hosts and guests. Airbnb has launched a new part of its website (airbnb.com/stories) that emphasizes the value of sharing personal stories. Airbnb's genuine concern for its neighborhood is exhibited by this strategy, which in turn draws more clients.

What characteristics define a fantastic narrative?
It would be best if you always attempted to satisfy these three conditions when telling a story:

- **Inform:** impart information and knowledge.
- **Engage**: Getting one's message across in a way that holds the listener's interest
- **Inspire**: To arouse curiosity and enthusiasm through creative thought.

We naturally transition between the three moods when our communication is vital. However, in the corporate world, we prioritize the first, only informing people with knowledge without inspiring them.

After you've memorized the story, it's time to work on your delivery and audience interaction, learning what makes your story compelling to others. The problem, the journey, and the resolution are the three main parts of any level.

- **The problem**: What problems have you discovered in your sector? What did the market need more of?
- **The journey**: How did you try to find a remedy for this issue? Explain the steps you took to bring your idea to fruition.
- **The solution**: In what ways will your business' offering revolutionize its field?

Tips for effective two-way communication in the workplace
A prevalent problem in the workplace is the underuse of two-way communication, which harms trust and employee engagement. Open communication inside internal systems is a must for successful modern businesses. The success of companies can be improved by emphasizing and facilitating two-way communication.

What is two-way communication?

The best analogy is a tennis match, with each player taking turns serving and returning the ball to the other. This constant dialogue keeps players interested and invested. Workplace conversational emphases have been linked to disengagement and low morale among workers. Enthusiastic, dedicated, and productive workers feel they collaborate with their superiors rather than report to them.

Two-way vs. one-way communication

Understanding the differences between two-way and one-way communication is critical for effectiveness in the job.

One-way communication	Two-way communication
Linear — All communication occurs between the sender and the recipient.	Circular — There is a constant two-way exchange of data between the sender and the recipient.
No response is expected or required.	Suggestions are welcomed and encouraged.
Used for passing along basic instructions, news, and announcements	Used for more involved communication, planning, and brainstorming
Takes less time	Takes longer
More formal	Less formal
Does not help the sender and recipient Communicate better with one another.	Boosts mutual comprehension and Closeness between sender and recipient
Examples: mass communication such as email blasts, newsletters, slideshows, radio or TV spots, whiteboard notes, etc.	Examples: Interactions between employees, whether in person, via video chat, or over the phone.

Justifications for fostering more interactive dialogue inside

The benefits of two-way communication for companies include preventing downward transmission and promoting transparent, unobstructed communication.

How to enhance two-way workplace communication

You can put yourself in the shoes of your target audience. Leaders need to know what motivates their staff and put themselves in their shoes to effectively inspire action. For starters, ask yourself some of these questions.

- What questions or reservations do my workers have?
- When trying to motivate your staff, knowing what information they have and what they're missing is essential.
- How is the top brass working to remove the obstacles that might make workers reluctant to back this initiative?
- What do I want my team to gain from this update in terms of knowledge, emotion, and action on my part as a leader? A more effective message can be crafted with the help of this question.

Choose or create the best channels

Motivating employees to speak up requires consideration of both the audience and the setting in which their words will be delivered. Before deciding whether to expand upon or utilize pre-existing channels, consider the resources at your disposal as well as the time, energy, and accessibility of your team. Even when the office is closed, staff members should have access to feedback mechanisms.

Gather and encourage feedback

A company's success relies heavily on its employees' enthusiasm and dedication. Leaders need to be responsive to employees' suggestions and inquiries by designating someone to handle problems and instituting programs like "employee ambassadors" or "communication liaisons" to facilitate regular feedback and information sharing.

Act on feedback

Employees who are invested in their work and its performance are said to be "engaged." Leaders should show appreciation for proposals by acting on them, publicizing the results of their efforts, and soliciting additional feedback. That establishes regular, reliable communication that inspires pride of ownership and appreciation among staff.

Advice on how to use humor to connect with your audience

The use of comedy can significantly increase an audience's interest and capacity for memory. A good impression of the speaker and their message is created. One's ability to captivate an audience through humor can make or ruin a presentation.

Including comedy in your speeches can:

- Establish a connection with your listeners, particularly at the beginning of your talk.
- Highlight and emphasize crucial ideas; humorous points are more likely to be remembered.
- Maintain your listeners' interest.
- Show some vulnerability to make yourself more approachable to the listener.
- Make people feel more at ease when dealing with unpleasant situations or answering tough questions.

WAYS TO LIGHTEN UP YOUR PRESENTATION

Incorporate it naturally

Make use of anecdotes and humorous stories based on actual events. They can help you connect with your audience and get your point across cleverly.

Integrate them into your argument, narrative, or topic

The anecdotes and humor should illuminate some truth or strengthen your argument. Remember that your listeners have come to benefit from your knowledge and experience; save their time with relevant anecdotes or jokes.

Adapt your humor to the people you're speaking to

To whom are you speaking, and can they appreciate your joke? In front of a group of tech-savvy millennials, your amusing anecdote about how you mistook "lol" for "lots of love" and then made a social faux pas might not land as well or be as entertaining. Get a feel for the audience's demographics, interests, and concerns, then use that information to craft jokes and anecdotes that will resonate with them. Not all marks are equally well-known. What resonates with one set of people or values may not do so with another.

Always avoid offensive humor

That may sound simple, but telling a crude joke is a quick way to lose your audience. It can turn off or alienate some of your audience, and it's hard to win them back once you've done that. Never resort to ethnic, racial, sexual, or otherwise offensive humor. Cringe, insult, extreme sarcasm, and black comedy should be avoided at all costs. Humor should be kept light and clean; crude jokes should be saved for stand-up comedians.

Do your cultural research

Knowing your audience's humor tastes and limits will help avoid offending them when sharing a joke. Ask a local if you want to know if the jokes land with the target audience. Sometimes, not even the best comedians can make their audiences laugh. Using comedy skillfully helps your audience connect with and learn from your message.

Motivational Story
Empowering staff
Crafting Success Through Effective Communication

The story of Peter serves as a compelling reminder of the intricate dance between skills, knowledge, and effective communication within the realm of leadership. As we dive deeper into leadership dynamics, let's explore how Peter's journey resonates with the core principles underpinning effective leadership.

Picture Peter, a diligent and brilliant worker who had, through sheer dedication, ascended the ranks to become a supervisor. His record of excellence and unwavering commitment was undoubtedly commendable, earning him this coveted role. The pivotal moment arrived when Peter's immediate boss, recognizing his capabilities, decided to test his mettle by entrusting him with a critical operation.

Peter was handed the reins as the seasoned supervisor took a much-needed day off. His knowledge of the company's operations was a wellspring of wisdom, allowing him to orchestrate an elaborate dance of preparation. With meticulous precision, he directed his team, organizing every minute of the task. From assembling products to coordinating utensils, every detail was methodically arranged. On the left are preparations for 300 passengers of Client A on the proper arrangements for the 400 passengers of Client B. An intricate tapestry of tasks and roles had been woven, poised for execution.

The culmination of their efforts was a feat to be celebrated. Peter's leadership had driven his team to fulfill all 700 services within the stipulated timeframe. Cheers of accomplishment echoed through the air, a testament to Peter's competence and his team's dedication.

Yet, within this tale of triumph lay a lesson etched in humility. As the deliveries commenced, an unforeseen slip occurred.

Amid the bustling coordination, Peter's skill in communicating with clarity faltered. The result: orders intended for Client A ended up with Client B, and vice versa. A simple miscommunication led to a complex web of unintended actions, highlighting the delicate interplay between knowledge, execution, and the often underestimated power of effective communication.

Leadership's essence is more than just encapsulated in proficiency within tasks. Instead, it rests on knowledge, strategic execution, and clear communication. Peter's story illuminates how even the most adept leaders can falter if they underestimate the significance of their words.

This narrative's resonance stems from its universality. Just as Peter's boss believed in his abilities, we, too, can fall into the trap of assuming that competence is synonymous with seamless leadership transitions. However, leadership is a dynamic journey that requires fostering, even for the most capable individuals. Peter's boss's oversight illustrates the necessity of providing consistent support, mentorship, and coaching to new leaders as they navigate the uncharted waters of their roles.

* * *

CHAPTER 5

DECISION-MAKING WITH STRUCTURED PROBLEM-SOLVING

Managers now play a significantly different role than they did a decade ago. Managers have transitioned from unseen backroom hands to front and center in modern businesses. Now that more people pay attention to managers, people expect them to be able to justify their decisions and actions. In any organization, the ability to make decisions is crucial. Employee frustration, stalled progress, and low morale are just a few of the adverse effects of a manager or supervisor who can't decide. However, the same negative results may occur if a company's management is prone to making rash decisions out of zeal or ignorance.

Skills Crucial to Good Leadership Decision-Making

Good leaders know how to keep their feelings in check long enough to make decisions that benefit everyone. They must think critically, maintain objectivity, and communicate appropriately in the face of change, uncertainty, and negative responses. The following are three crucial decision-making skills for leaders:

Logical reasoning

Executives must carefully consider all relevant information before making strategic decisions. Leaders need to reason through the benefits and drawbacks of their planned actions. To make rational and objective choices, leaders must first develop insight into themselves and their motivations.

Problem-solving

Decisions about the future of a company, its staff, and many other factors all require the problem-solving skills of its leaders. They must do more than assess the issue; they must also consider the big picture, factoring in things like deadlines, probable setbacks, and strategic priorities. After collecting data, it's time to analyze it thoroughly.

Emotional intelligence

Leaders who can't recognize, control, and express positive emotions are less likely to make wise choices. To make good choices, you need to develop your emotional intelligence. Leadership coaching can aid in making intelligent and profitable choices by ensuring that new habits are compatible with existing pressures and responsibilities. Enhance workplace decision-making by implementing this strategy.

Making better decisions as a leader is a skill that can be honed and refined in many settings. Since these improve under the guidance of an experienced leadership coach,

- Deal with the most demanding choices first: Procrastination is one of the most significant obstacles to sound decision-making. Those anxious or stressed are more likely to put off making choices. When issues are dealt with promptly, they can be fixed with minimal impact on business as usual.
- It's in a leader's best interest to be well-informed before making a decision, so it's recommended that

they do their research. Understanding the decision's context and relevant elements requires knowing what factors are at play.

- Don't make snap judgments based on your feelings; doing so will only lead to bad decisions. If a choice or action needs to be taken, but leaders can't be objective, it's usually best to wait. Think about the main facts rather than your sentiments, and if you need more time to get your head around everything, don't hesitate to ask for it.

How to Make Decisions

Whether simple or complex, decisions have consequences for businesses and their projects. Managers and those aspiring to management roles must pay close attention to detail and fully grasp the processes of making sound judgments. To make wiser managerial choices, consider the following decision-making steps:

Determine which course of action is required.

Find out as much as you can so you can make educated choices. If the problem has been defined, open-ended questions can be asked for more information. It's easier to tackle a problem with multiple solutions if you break it down into smaller pieces.

Review relevant information

You can generate ideas once you've settled on a course of action. To make a good choice, you need to consider all the data. When reviewing a large amount of data, confusion is inevitable. Use tools like flowcharts and colorful Post-it notes to help you stay on track. You must carefully place only one in a pile of hundreds of papers. Involving other team members in accumulating pertinent information is a fantastic way to gain new perspectives on a problem.

Think about possible alternatives

Is there a finite number of ways to go about making this choice? You've likely thought about many possibilities now that you've evaluated the data thoroughly. Many options may exist, but there is a better time to choose the best. In its place, you should put your energy into compiling a list of potential outcomes through inquiry and response.

Weigh your evidence

Assess the advantages and disadvantages of each idea you've generated. Consider the decisions your competitors have made and the outcomes they've achieved. Analyze the pros and cons of every option under consideration. Deliberate on the implications for your team members and other parties impacted by your decision. What adjustments will they need to adapt to? Ensure you reach this stage, enabling you to make an informed choice that will propel you forward with confidence.

Choose the solution

The time has come for you to make a final choice. Examine the evidence and contemplate your options. The next step is for you to choose. Have faith in yourself; you can make this decision.

Take action

The final phase is carrying out your choice. Make a strategy that guarantees your personal and professional success. Strategic planning might be time-consuming, but the rewards of a good decision, like happy coworkers and a clear head, are only realized through the effective implementation of the plan.

Reflect on your decision

Reflecting on your decision-making process is the key to internalizing your work and attaining your goals. Reviewing one's actions, both good and bad, helps one grow as a person. Possible answers may be found more quickly if people work together and use what is already available. Performing a post-mortem analysis can help you better prepare for making difficult choices. Consider this and use it to your advantage when preparing for upcoming tests.

DATA ANALYSIS

Data analysis is the process of gathering information and examining it logically and statistically. Insights for strategic and operational decision-making are gleaned from data using analytics technologies. Combining your knowledge of quantitative and qualitative research methods gives you a solid foundation to build in-depth analytical reports. The most effective ways of data analysis are:

Collaborate on your needs

Before diving into analysis or honing in on specific methodologies, it's essential to sit down as a team and figure out what your crucial campaign or strategic goals are, as well as obtain a grounding understanding of the kind of knowledge that can help you advance or offer the vision you need to expand your business.

Establish your questions

Consider the questions you must resolve after deciding what you want to accomplish. That is a crucial strategy because it will form the basis of your success. To ensure your data is applicable, you must ask the proper questions during data analysis.

Data democratization

By effectively linking data from different sources, data democratization grants unlimited access to all employees. Crucial steps in data analytics techniques include extracting data in several formats, doing cross-database analysis, and identifying essential sources. For efficient decision-making and sharing within the company, it is crucial to collect insights organizationally.

Think of governance

Protecting sensitive information and avoiding data breaches make data governance necessary in business and research settings. Methods, functions, and guidelines are all part of this plan to maximize data utilization and advance organizational objectives. The protection of sensitive data and the effectiveness of analysis depend on well-defined responsibilities and access controls.

Clean up your data

Cleaning up data from numerous sources can be exhausting and lead to erroneous conclusions. Eliminating duplicate observations, missing codes, and poor formatting is essential for precise insights. Additionally, incorrect characters and grammatical problems should be removed from text data like customer reviews and surveys. The end goal is to keep the business from drawing any unwarranted inferences.

Set your KPIs

Once you have established your sources, cleansed your data, and developed clear-cut questions you want your insights to answer, setting key performance indicators (KPIs) can help you track, measure, and impact your progress in various crucial areas. Key performance indicators are essential in qualitative and quantitative studies alike. Please pay attention to this as one of the approaches to data analysis.

Omit useless data

Exploring raw data and using KPIs as a reference can help you apply data analysis tools and methodologies efficiently. Eliminating extra details from the data is essential for drilling down into significant trends and patterns. Any data, measurements, or statistics that don't contribute to achieving company objectives or KPI management strategies should be discarded.

Create a plan for managing your data

Creating a data governance roadmap is not required but is essential for long-term data analysis strategies. Iteration and expansion are possible with well-thought-out roadmaps. Spending effort here will improve the efficiency and effectiveness of your analysis procedures, elevating them to the ranks of the most potent data analysis strategies now in use.

Integrate technology

While there are various approaches to data analysis, integrating appropriate decision support tools and technology is crucial for analytical success in a business environment. The best way to get the most out of your business's most valuable insights is to integrate the correct technology into your data analysis process to prevent fragmenting them.

Answer your questions

You may quickly answer your most important business concerns by following the procedures mentioned above, working with the appropriate technology, and cultivating a unified organizational culture where everyone sees the value of data analysis and digital intelligence. Data visualization is a powerful tool for making complex data concepts understandable to a broader audience inside an organization.

Visualize your data

Online data visualization is a potent tool because it allows you to tell a story with your measurements, facilitating the extraction of relevant insights that aid in expanding a business across the board.

Use caution with your interpretation

Since businesses typically must integrate information from numerous sources, the interpretation phase requires special attention to detail to provide accurate results. As a guide, I've compiled a list of three mistakes you should never make while analyzing your data:

- **Correlation vs. causation:** The human brain has a natural tendency to look for patterns, which can lead to erroneous conclusions about cause and effect. To prevent this from happening, one should rely on data rather than intuition, and in the absence of such evidence, one should settle for correlation.
- **Confirmation bias:** Confirmation bias occurs when someone selects and reinterprets data to fit their preconceived idea while ignoring or downplaying contrary information. That can cause erroneous inferences and bad choices in the commercial world. Avoid jumping to conclusions about the project's outcome by testing and refuting hypotheses, discussing findings, and passing judgment early on.
- **Statistical significance:** Analysis of statistical significance, which varies by sample size and field, is essential for making sound business decisions.

Build a narrative
The human mind is extraordinarily receptive to compelling storytelling. Doing so will make your analytical work easier to understand and apply across the board, giving more people in your business a chance to benefit from your findings.

Consider autonomous technology
Autonomous technologies like artificial intelligence (AI) and machine learning (ML) have greatly aided our understanding of conducting more effective data analysis. These innovations are currently shaking up the analytical sector.

Share the load
With the proper software and dashboards, you can present your analytics in a way that is easy to understand and action-

able for virtually everyone in your organization. When everyone on staff adopts a data-driven approach to their work, you'll stimulate the company's growth in ways you never thought possible. This kind of teamwork is crucial when it comes to data analysis skills.

Data analysis tools

It's crucial to have access to the proper hardware and software for thorough data analysis. Let me briefly describe four types of data analysis tools that your business can find helpful.

- **Business Intelligence:** Data from various sources can be processed in any format using BI tools. In addition to keeping an eye on and analyzing your data for actionable insights, you can also use this to create dynamic reports and dashboards for visualizing your key performance indicators (KPIs).
- **Statistical analysis:** Regression analysis, predictive analysis, and statistical modeling are only some of the complicated statistical procedures made possible by the software aimed at scientists, statisticians, market researchers, and mathematicians.
- **SQL Consoles:** In relational databases, SQL is a popular language for working with structured data. Data scientists favor these kinds of tools because of how well they reveal hidden value in extensive collections.
- **Data Visualization:** You can use these programs to make sense of your data by visualizing it in tables, charts, and maps.

Refine your process constantly

The final step may seem unnecessary to some, but it's easy to overlook if you're confident that everything else has been taken care of. Once the necessary results have been extracted, the project should always be looked back to determine where and how it may be improved. The vast array of methods presented here demonstrates the complexity of data analysis and the need for ongoing improvement. Consequently, it would be best always to push yourself to improve.

Arguments for including your team in strategic planning

You have to make a lot of choices as a manager. The pressure to make a decision can affect anyone, no matter their decision-making experience. The more at stake, the more difficult it is to make a call. It's in our nature to play it safe, even if that means passing up a great chance. Here are the reasons why you should include your team in strategic planning:

Making decisions as a group saves time

You want to put your choice into action immediately. That makes sense since you'll enjoy the benefits of your choice even sooner. Your company's bottom line will increase if everything goes according to plan. To ensure a smooth and efficient rollout:

- Get everyone on board who will be responsible for implementing the final solution early on.
- Create a decision-making group that represents a range of expertise, experience, and perspectives.
- Create well-defined objectives and brainstorm potential approaches.

You encourage creative thinking among your staff

It's only sometimes the best strategy for a team to wait for unanimity. Promote robust discussion by asking probing questions and inviting counterarguments. Pose thought-provoking questions and foster alternative points of view to inspire the development of novel approaches. Participate actively and refrain from being indifferent to reaching an agreement.

You Increase Team Engagement

Participation in decision-making has been shown to increase team motivation. Every day, you deliberate over 35,000 different options. If you're alone, that's a lot to take on. Involving people shows you appreciate their input, and employees who feel their opinions matter are more invested in their work. Teams with involved members in turn:

- Feel less pressure and tension.
- A higher chance of staying in the company's employ.
- Better outcomes can be attained.

The more decisions you delegate to your team, the more they may contribute their skills, knowledge, and experience to the company. Employees become more invested in the group's success, and as a result, they are more likely to contribute to the organization's success.

You Improve Team Collaboration

Collective decision-making strengthens a team. Most employers place a high value on the ability to collaborate with others. Communication is a powerful tool for improving teamwork. However, it isn't always a breeze. The inability to work together or communicate effectively is the root cause of about 90% of workplace failures. Participate in group discussions. If you do this, you'll be giving them a chance to:

- Talk about your thoughts.
- Encourage mutual education.
- Cooperate to achieve your objectives.

The best way to eliminate silos is to handle decision-making as a group. You may find some redundancies in your team that you can eliminate to stop wasting time and money.

You Identify Your Blind Spots

Do you know what your best qualities are? What about your weakest? It's easier to make good choices when you have a firm grasp of your own personal leadership style, skills, and shortcomings. The chances of a decision's success increase as a result. Incorporate the group's input and

- Extend your horizons.
- Develop a better understanding of who you are.
- Gain experience in management roles.

You Support Team Development

Giving your team a voice will help them succeed. Does your group value personal and professional development? Then, prioritize group decision-making. Your encouragement will inspire your team to:

- Increase your involvement in the company.
- Learn more about the history of their field and the significance of their work.
- Those linguistic abilities must be honed.

All of these enhancements will make your team more productive. As a result, your group has a better chance of achieving the lofty goals set by your firm.

You Build a Stronger Team

Collective decision-making improves collaboration. Individuals differ from one another in a wide variety of ways. These characteristics tend to become more pronounced under pressure. It's easier to solve issues when team members of all types can work together. When people work together, they make better decisions. Each new challenge you overcome as a group brings you closer together.

Put only a little stock in your experiences to make wise choices. Although it's helpful, experience is no guarantee against making mistakes. Staying in your managerial bubble without soliciting employee feedback increases the likelihood that you will make poor choices.

The Importance of Time in Decision Making

Management decision-making is essential since it determines a business's course of action and outcomes. It requires making judgments and responding to data. Making calculated choices promptly is necessary to accomplish goals to avoid a crisis. Three factors—time, availability, and implementation—affect the decision-making process and highlight the importance of time. Making a choice requires considering many angles and taking several steps.

Decision times are greatly affected by a person's level of knowledge and experience, which can be skewed by both past events and environmental factors. Deliberate mental processing, including consideration of contextual factors, is required for decision-making. Successful outcomes depend on timing because it facilitates the visualization of vital elements and the decision-maker's coordination of pivotal key points. Delaying decisions to collect additional data or process the information is only sometimes a good idea because it can cause you to eliminate the best options due to indecision. The environment constantly shifts; therefore, it's only occasionally safe to base decisions on the past.

On the other hand, looking back at prior choices and learning from them might help shape future ones. Aspects of time are situationally specific, but they all play a vital role in decision-making. When making a choice, it's common to have to make a compromise between speed and quality. Time is a significant factor in shaping preferences, and as people's exposure to and familiarity with various options evolve, so do their tastes.

Decision-making is a process that unfolds over time

Some decisions are quick and intuitive, while others require more time to process the information. Decisions that call for extensive analysis and consideration of potential outcomes take time. If time is considered, the choice can be either static or dynamic. The time required, the best time to decide, and any structural shifts are all factors in emotional decision-making. The decision-making process and the decision-making job are considered to be static.

Long-term decisions that affect subsequent ones are viewed as active. The speed with which a system evolves affects how quickly its stakeholders must make decisions. The human perforator acts perfectly when needed, despite often poor performance and a lack of response to the speed of change. Therefore, time is essential for decision-makers.

Time, both as a commodity and a connected quality

The process of decision-making is very demanding and requires one's undivided concentration. Having the ability to make rapid judgments when time is of the essence might be challenging. The limited time available affects Decisions and how they're made. Negative information can have a diversity of effects, including but not limited to reducing the use of compensatory choice strategies, increasing the likelihood of forgetting essential data, leading to erroneous judgment and evaluation, narrowing the range of alternatives and dimensions considered, elevating chosen options, prompting defensive reactions, and so on.

Time limitations are a crucial task variable that pronounced affects the judgment call. Decision-makers may resort to less stringent, faster, but less accurate methods when time is of the essence. When confronted with a moderate time crunch, decision-makers reduce their analysis, whereas those facing a severe time crunch turn to qualitative approaches.

Time constraints require a multifaceted approach. When making decisions under time constraints, it's easy to make rash choices. The former calls for quick thinking and action due to time restrictions, whereas the latter suggests laziness. Understanding how and why time pressure impacts decision-making is vital in the real world, especially in times of crisis.

Story

Cultivating Empowerment: Nurturing Growth Through Autonomy

Within the spectrum of leadership styles, the narrative of my journey under the guidance of an unconventional yet empowering manager comes to the forefront. This chapter unfurls the subtle art of fostering autonomy within a team, enriching our understanding of how leadership can elevate performance by embracing innovation and initiative.

Imagine the backdrop of a burgeoning catering empire, masterminded by a self-made entrepreneur who, in his late 40s, yearned to redirect his focus to his true passion: crafting visionary businesses and pioneering the products he ardently believed in. This visionary, my boss, envisioned a future where his domain encompassed innovation rather than maintenance. To this end, he sought a maintenance manager to free him from operational minutiae.

My appointment came with skepticism. My background in civil engineering marked a divergence from the catering realm, and apprehension lingered over whether I could transition seamlessly into this novel role. Surprisingly, my boss took a leap of faith, granting me a proverbial canvas to paint my ideas. "What do you think?" he inquired during those early days, casting aside the expected scrutinizing gaze. His interest in my insights initially struck me as a trial, a litmus test of my capabilities.

The turning point manifested when I presented my concept for a comprehensive maintenance manual designed to extend equipment longevity and empower the production team. Expecting a barrage of queries and critique, I was taken aback when he said, "If you believe it can work, give it a shot." A nod of approval was all I needed to embark on this venture, a testament to the trust he vested in me.

As weeks progressed, an atmosphere of autonomy enveloped me. My boss, astutely realizing the potential of nurturing ownership, allowed me to flourish independently. He entrusted me with the reins while sporadic guidance was offered in passing. Frequent emails were my conduit to maintain transparency and seek advice without compromising my newfound autonomy.

The crescendo of this story arrived through the voice of our HR manager, who unveiled a candid truth: She had selected me not just for my expertise but for my potential. The virtue of autonomy found its champion in my boss, who recognized that micromanagement could eclipse innovation. This revelation liberated me further, allowing my autonomy to blossom and my initiatives to flourish.

The pinnacle of affirmation arrived post-launch of the maintenance manual, a resounding success that reverberated beyond our sphere. An email materialized, bestowing me the title of "the appropriate person for the job." In this story's tapestry, this moment crystallizes the power of empowerment, illustrating that when leaders bestow trust and autonomy upon their team, remarkable feats can emerge.

* * *

CHAPTER 6
EMPOWERING THROUGH DELEGATION AND COACHING

Tasks and initiatives can be delegated to other members of the team. One of the keys to being an effective manager is learning when and how to trust. Delegating tasks helps you complete important work and allows your team members to engage in more engaging lessons. Effective delegation is a crucial factor in developing team abilities and individual talents. Working with a coach in the workplace can help boost productivity, efficiency, and accuracy on both an individual and group basis. We will talk about both delegation and coaching in this chapter.

Successful coaching techniques that propel teams to success Organizational goals are more challenging when workers need more leadership and team cohesion. Businesses with a firm grasp of their customers' wants, needs, and contributions may increase customer retention, productivity, and bottom line.

What Is Coaching a Team?
Coaching is more than just coordinating workers. It also encourages them to capitalize on their unique skills and strengths. Executives and managers often start the coaching

process, which leads to a more welcoming workplace culture. Coaching is not mentoring; it gives people the tools they need to achieve their goals. One way to help employees and improve one's management skills is to hone one's coaching skills. Here is how you can do it:

Know Your employees

To be an effective leader, you need to know your team inside and out, including their biggest motivators and deepest fears. Regular self-evaluations and personality tests can better understand employees' strengths and short-comings.

Foster Transparency

Openness, trust, and partnerships are all bolstered when people feel they can speak their minds. Fostering an environment of free dialogue and discussion among workers by answering pressing questions

- How often do I let others into my life to get to know me?
- Have I clarified to my team members what I value and why I work hard?
- How lucid and consistent am I in my decision-making?
- When I make a mistake or discover a gap in my understanding, do I communicate that to my coworkers?

You can't ask your team to do anything you wouldn't do yourself, and the same holds for leadership. Show the way.

Collaboration is key

People have a natural tendency to compete with one another. As a result, office rivalries are often unavoidable. By discouraging unhealthy competition, encouraging collaboration, and celebrating group triumphs rather than individual success, you may develop a culture where members thrive as a team and are driven to rely on one another.

Establish Clear Aims and targets

The process of developing objectives and goals through strategic planning is essential. Start by taking a step back and looking at the big picture, then get people brainstorming and using their unique skills. Create a schedule with key dates and metrics to track progress and evaluate team performance.

Celebrate Success

Motivating and inspiring your staff overtime requires celebrating their successes and achievements. Motivation and morale can be boosted by holding celebrations for work anniversaries, individual accomplishments, professional advancements, and team victories.

Build Mutual trust

Trust must be mutually given and received; doors must always be open. There must be an open dialogue, and the coach must not pass judgment. Encourage honesty, keep your door open, and show that you care about the team's progress.

Pave the Way for Success

With proper preparation, your employees can perform at peak levels. Therefore, make sure your team has all the tools they need to do their jobs well, including the proper education, hardware, software, resources, tactics, and materials, and address any gaps as soon as possible.

Share Constructive feedback

Employee coaching that successfully reveals strengths, flaws, and development opportunities relies heavily on feedback. The ability to articulate ideas, hone one's abilities, and take criticism from peers is crucial.

Ask for feedback

The most successful and competent instructors are also highly teachable. To help your employees fulfill the performance and conduct standards you've established together, solicit input on how you might improve your coaching of them in group settings and one-on-one. Be receptive, adaptable, and objective during the discussion.

Manage Inter-Team Disputes

Inadequate employee participation or mild bullying undermines the benefits of team building. Constant vigilance and response are required, as is the establishment of measures to forestall further occurrences.

Advice for supervisors on how to delegate properly

Managers benefit from delegation since it frees their time to focus on high-impact tasks and increases employee engagement. While the ability to trust is a crucial leadership talent, it can take time for newly promoted managers to acquire.

Why do we need to delegate?

Tasks and projects can be delegated within a team so that work is shared more equitably or that team members can focus on what matters most to them personally or professionally. Delegating tasks effectively not only speeds up the completion of high-impact work but also gives team members a chance to engage in engaging projects, which helps everyone grow individually and collectively.

Why is it helpful to delegate?

You must learn to delegate tasks to get the most out of your day and show your team that you trust them. To avoid burnout and overwork, it is vital to learn to delegate responsibilities to your team members in a way that takes advantage of their strengths. Leading well and assigning appropriate tasks can provide your team with invaluable learning experiences. New team skills can be developed, and professional growth can be tracked with the aid of delegation.

Why don't people delegate more?

If you're a first-time manager, delegating tasks can be highly challenging. Why some people have a hard time delegating:

- Being concerned that explaining the process may take longer than actually performing it
- I am figuring out what tasks should be completed first.
- Seeks out challenging endeavors in which to engage.
- Regret giving others additional work to do.
- Who else should I ask to help out?
- Seek to play a pivotal role on the squad.

When to delegate work

Concerns to address before handing off work:

- Is there a different team member who would benefit more from taking on this task?
- Can this task be delegated to someone with the necessary knowledge and experience?
- Is there room for improvement and advancement in this position?
- When might we expect to see a repeat of this task?
- Do I have enough time to train the other person, respond to their inquiries, and review their work effectively?
- Is this something I must prioritize because of its importance to the company?
- How might a setback affect the project's outcome?
- Can we afford to redo the job if it turns out to be subpar?

Answering "yes" to these questions is not mandatory before delegating tasks. The best duties to entrust can be identified by asking oneself the questions mentioned earlier.

TIPS FOR DELEGATING WORK

Learning to assign tasks makes you a more effective manager and gives your team members more opportunities to work on exciting projects. To get started with delegation, consider the following guidelines:

Identify work to delegate

It's only sometimes feasible to delegate work, especially when it involves matters of strategic or business-essential importance. Consider the task's significance and potential outcomes before handing it off. Even if another team member has the requisite experience or skill set to do a crucial assignment, it is still your responsibility to ensure a successful outcome. The following are examples of tasks that are appropriate for delegation:

- Find someone who can devote time and effort to the task, and you'll save yourself a lot of hassle in the long run.
- If a team member has expressed interest in learning a new skill or improving upon an existing one, consider whether there is any work you can delegate to them that will allow them to do so.
- Assigning tasks directly relevant to an employee's professional development is a great strategy to foster effective delegation.

Practice letting go

First-time managers and leaders may find delegating difficult because it requires them to entrust others with responsibility. If you're nervous about starting a significant endeavor, begin with something easy. It takes time to master delegation, so be patient with yourself and your team as you get there. You can help your team members grow professionally and get more done by giving them assignments.

Clarify priorities

Tasks can be delegated more effectively when their relative importance and complexity are known. Depending on the nature of the work, you may choose to complete urgent tasks personally or assign them. Prioritizing and finishing high-impact tasks is simplified when their significance in reaching team and company goals is clear. By centralizing team efforts in a project management application or other agreed-upon repository, you can easily see who is responsible for what and when.

Recognize and capitalize on everyone's unique skills

When you delegate, you put a team member in a position to succeed by giving them tasks that match their expertise and giving them room to grow in those areas. To accomplish this, discuss with each team member one-on-one and learn about their areas of expertise and interest.

Provide context and guidance

Ensure the individual you're passing work off to has all they need to succeed before you give it off. Some examples are:

- Instructions for carrying out the assigned tasks
- When the assigned task needs to be completed
- What resources will be required?
- What the assignment's priorities, goals, and expected outcomes are
- What other tasks are related to the one being assigned?

Invest in training

Team members can benefit from taking on non-personal tasks when they are delegated to do so. Training is an expense that pays for itself through improved efficiency and productivity.

Building time management skills and opening up new prospects are two benefits of delegating work. Problem-solving, decision-making, and the confidence to take on challenges and succeed as a team are all honed through training.

Prioritize communication and feedback

When tasks are delegated, it allows for more two-way contact and feedback. Ensure the person you've charged to has someone to ask questions about and set up regular check-ins. Make suggestions for upcoming work and encourage free-from-inquiry to boost productivity. Since learning to delegate effectively is an acquired ability, checking in for feedback regularly is essential.

Focus on results

The person you delegate to may complete the task in a way that differs from your approach, and that's perfectly acceptable. Just ensure that you entrust the team member with the responsibility of shaping the process and concentrating on achieving the ultimate result. In addition to showing that you have faith in their abilities to get the job done, this also gives them a chance to hone their craft. Avoid lengthy explanations and push for independent process development among team members.

Trust, but verify

Assign tasks to team members and give them the room and resources they need to succeed. Maintain consistent contact and show trust by asking if they need any support. Take ownership of the results and set up a review process or time for follow-up for tasks that have been delegated.

Give credit once the work is completed

When tasks are distributed adequately among team members, everyone can learn and grow while contributing to meaningful endeavors. Never claim credit for someone else's effort. Instead, give praise to the team member who did it. Take note of the team member's efforts and show gratitude for their job.

Delegated and done

As well as improving your management abilities, delegating tasks helps everyone on your team advance in their careers. Ensure your coworkers have everything they need to complete the assigned task successfully after you've entrusted it.

Facilitating your team's success at work

Working as a team has its advantages and disadvantages, but ultimately leads to success because of the unique perspectives and experiences each member brings to the table. However, it is paramount to guarantee that every team member feels like they belong. Whether you're the team's leader or a team member, this section will help you understand why team support is crucial and what you can do to provide it.

Why is teamwork essential?

Coworkers must have each other's backs at the office. That is due to many factors:

- It improves both productivity and originality. When people put their heads together, great things can happen. Furthermore, a study indicated that diverse teams were up to 35% more creative and outperformed their less varied counterparts in terms of both innovation and performance.
- It's a stress reliever. Successful cooperation increases interpersonal relationships, higher morale, and less stress.
- Skill development is facilitated. Everyone benefits when everyone contributes their unique skills to the collaborative effort. Teamwork allows individuals to pool resources, gain new insights, and boost efficiency.

What are the barriers to an effective team?

Some obstacles may stand in the way of a collection of people joining together to form an effective team. Recognizing these roadblocks is a critical first step in providing support in the workplace. Among these are:

- Inadequate verbal exchanges. Good communication skills are crucial to team success. Those with trouble communicating their wants, desires, and emotions need help working together effectively.
- Undefined outcomes. It is challenging to progress if everyone is tugging in separate directions. With a common goal, teams can maintain focus and cohesion.
- A failure to take charge. A leader's ability to inspire and direct their team is one of their many strengths. Groups are likely to succeed with these qualities, especially among management.
- No one is taking responsibility. Delineating responsibilities and understanding each team member's role are imperative. Without these factors, the likelihood of experiencing conflicts and a lack of unity increases.

How to support your team at work

No matter your position on the team, you should always do everything you can to assist the group and its leader. Here are eleven strategies, some of which emphasize personal development while others emphasize helping others more directly. Your team's efficiency and effectiveness at the office could benefit from these suggestions.

Communicate regularly

In-person or online, open and honest communication is crucial to productive teamwork. It's a great way to improve communication skills and keep everyone up-to-date. Managers and leaders are responsible for keeping everyone in the loop about what needs to be done and where the team can improve. At the same time, those not in management should focus on building relationships and giving people a safe space to share their thoughts and opinions. Effective communication can only build relationships and open dialogue between group members.

Check-in regularly

Sometimes, there are better strategies than a hands-off approach to teamwork. Consistent get-togethers for project updates and individual growth can maintain a team's cohesiveness. Leaders are responsible for facilitating regular feedback and support for their teams while encouraging each member to participate in their development actively. To foster a more cooperative and productive work environment, mental check-ins and mindfulness techniques can be used to recognize and evaluate one's feelings and experiences.

Be inclusive

When working with a varied group of people, it's essential to recognize and appreciate everyone's unique qualities. Rejecting ideas that don't fit oneself can be demoralizing and tense. Acknowledging and dealing with differing viewpoints and conflicts respectfully can lead to learning opportunities and beneficial compromise, so it's important to remember this. Everyone should speak up and attempt to include others.

Learn to prioritize

Having a plan in place for how to get the most important things done can reduce stress in the workplace for everyone involved. The workplace is diverse because it relies on the unique expertise of each employee to accomplish its objectives. If everyone puts forth their best effort, efficiency and good judgment for the team will increase.

Empower others

Helping your team includes enabling others to help themselves. It entails giving others space to form their opinions, create their plans, and act on those plans according to their best judgment. If you want to help people flourish, delegating tasks, setting limits, and providing constructive feedback are essential daily activities. While leaders play an important part, everyone can help create a more collaborative and creative workplace by encouraging open dialogue and new ideas.

Work on your emotional intelligence

Understanding, controlling, and identifying one's emotions are all components of emotional intelligence, a highly sought-after "soft skill" in today's competitive job market. It's a great way to make friends and work well with others. Improved cooperation and productivity are the results of high emotional intelligence. One can learn from others by thinking about one's work surroundings and accepting personal responsibility for one's conduct.

Set reasonable goals

Having shared goals and expectations is imperative when working remotely so everyone can rally around. Burnout and frustration can occur if there is too much pressure to achieve goals. Each member should be responsible for establishing their objectives, but it's essential to have goals that everyone can work toward. That encourages personal responsibility, professional development, and agency.

Take breaks together

In the workplace, breaks are essential because of their positive effects on workers' ability to think critically, generate new ideas, and get more done. Relationships, group cohesion, and individual inspiration all benefit from them. Breaks regularly can help keep the team motivated.

Focus on well-being

Supporting your team at work requires serious consideration for their health and happiness. It encourages healthy work-life balance and candid conversations on mental health and well-being. When people prioritize well-being, the workplace becomes happier and more productive. Mindfulness and encouraging people to think about their well-being are two methods that can be used to accomplish this.

Promote growth

All employees should feel supported in pursuing personal and professional development in the workplace. Effective leadership development includes coaching, courses, and on-the-job instruction. Team members can learn from each other and work together to find solutions if encouraged to share their skills. A positive work environment promotes learning and development at all levels of responsibility through inquiry, comprehension, and instruction.

Success in Business Depends on Promoting Employee Independence

Employees trusted to make decisions and act independently from their superiors are given more freedom at work. The burden on workers is relieved, and they are more likely to be happy, productive, creative, innovative, and grow as individuals when an environment of autonomy is fostered. This method results in increased productivity in the workplace and a more inspiring brand of leadership.

Support a Growth mindset

Developing an independent culture encourages a growth mindset. If Employees want to succeed in the workplace, they must be able to adopt a growth mindset and look beyond their current circumstances. In many ways, but notably in learning new abilities, ambition and motivation like these are vital.

Build a Culture of trust

Leaders should delegate responsibilities and allow workers to shine to build team trust. Avoiding setbacks and guaranteeing that workers can handle challenges can be accomplished by starting small and expanding responsibilities and independence as workers prove their mettle.

Let Employees Do Things Their Way

Leaders should push for a culture of autonomy where workers are trusted to figure out where they fit in and how to get their jobs done without constant supervision. Companies like Google and Amazon show how a workplace culture that promotes independence, trust, and teamwork can improve operations.

Methods to Celebrate Professional Achievement

The traditional idea of success at work has changed as people learn to balance their professional and personal lives. Employers must acknowledge and reward intergenerational successes if they want to promote social connections. It is essential to success to recognize and celebrate these accomplishments.

When an employee achieves a goal at work, why should they receive recognition?

Here are the top four reasons why you, your team, and your company should celebrate success in the workplace:

1. Help you assess the quality of your efforts

It serves as a helpful reminder of the team's objectives and the work they've accomplished. They can take stock of how far their efforts have brought them. Understanding what went right and where they need to make improvements is helpful.

2. Foster Interpersonal Connections

When a group gets together to celebrate a job well done, they strengthen their relationships with one another and the company. Relationships and trust are maintained as a result.

3. Offer Essential Relief

Changing the focus of your team's efforts from "work" to "celebration" can infuse everyone with fresh enthusiasm and productivity.

4. Serve as a Morale Booster

The motivation of your team can be significantly increased by celebrating its achievements. When workers know their contributions are appreciated, they tend to work more. Communicating the company's success to employees is a proven method of boosting morale.

ADVICE FOR QUICKLY CLIMBING THE CORPORATE LADDER

There should never be a time when you say "No" to learning

It would be best if you encouraged a culture of lifelong learning among your staff. It's a great way to help them hone their abilities and skills. Once you've assessed their advantages and disadvantages, you can have confidence in their abilities. It will further their growth and the team's overall effectiveness.

Maintain a positive perspective

Keep a level head whether things are going great or wrong. Don't get angry or harsh with your staff. Your team's low morale and output are likely due to your state of mind. Instead, do your research to identify appropriate feedback loops.

Encourage positive stories!

Tell success stories about specific employees who went above and beyond to help customers or develop an outstanding new feature. The result is an improved mood at work and more potent bonds among employees. Set aside time at regular staff meetings to discuss and recount such experiences.

Take charge of finding solutions to issues

When things aren't going as planned, it's common for managers to give employees more autonomy. When they succeed, some people like to claim credit for other people's efforts. It would be best to take the lead on accountability, even when things get complicated. To be successful in your career, you need to have the innate capacity to find solutions to problems and to lead when it matters most.

Be receptive and open to feedback

Leaders who don't take the time to listen to their followers will find themselves surrounded by silent followers. Finding the right balance between giving orders and hearing out employees is essential in management. While you may provide broad direction, it is ultimately the work of your staff to bring a concept to fruition. You may lose touch with the vision's development and process if you don't pay attention and actively listen.

Recognize achievements

If you are a manager or leader who wishes to recognize achievement on the job, think about the following:

- How can we best show appreciation for coworkers?
- When is the right time to show gratitude?
- How may appreciation be best shown?

Don't be shy about praising a team player who has excelled in their position. It's not just for morale but also to get the team fired up about the bigger picture.

Make time to meet your team

You can do more for morale around the office if you make an effort to regularly meet with employees face-to-face, both in group settings and one-on-one chats. Businesses should make it a point to celebrate employees' achievements regularly to enhance morale, build the team, create ties, and increase participation. Here are a few excellent reasons for rejoicing over a job well done:

- A profitable quarter
- Achieving a goal or finishing a project
- Work-related milestones
- Obtaining results, such as sales targets,
- Gaining more positive feedback from clients

A Tale of Adaptation, Empowerment and Delegation
The year 2020 ushered in an unparalleled challenge—the pandemic. Against this backdrop, my journey led me to the helm of a multinational company in a South American nation. Little did I realize that my ascent to the general manager role would mirror the company's transition and underscore the essence of adaptability and growth.

In the wake of this transition, a reconfiguration rippled through the company. Just as the world redefined its norms, positions that had stood firm for years underwent a recalibration. In their wake, the trusted allies of former leaders emerged as the torchbearers of this new era, tasked with steering each domain towards uncharted horizons. This metamorphosis echoed a broader narrative: Leadership was evolving, requiring everyone to navigate uncharted waters with poise.

Angie, a beacon of dedication recognized throughout the company for her tireless efforts and unwavering commitment, stood at the heart of this transformation. However, the winds of change carried with them an undertow of trepidation as she embraced her new role. The influx of novel responsibilities intermingling with her existing tasks quickly became a storm threatening to consume her. The clarity that once marked her approach became blurred, her assertiveness faltered, and the dynamics of her relationships underwent a metamorphosis—from peer to leader.

This turbulence translated into her department's performance, which spiraled downwards. The synergy she had orchestrated seemed to fade, and a disheartening narrative unfolded. Yet, amidst this turmoil, Angie and I developed a bond of trust and transparency. Vulnerability became a conduit for shared understanding, allowing her to express her uncertainties and challenges. Thus, the transformation journey began—exploring the factors undermining her potential.

Peeling back the layers, we uncovered a divergence between her tasks and the new role's demands. Operational intricacies, which had been second nature, now overshadowed the strategic compass her leadership necessitated. This incongruity sparked a pivot towards a recalibrated focus on management, strategic planning, goal-setting, and vigilant oversight.

Further exploration revealed another pivotal aspect: the art of delegation. Angie's noble attempt at entrusting tasks to her team inadvertently relinquished indispensable elements of her new responsibilities. Precious facets of her role that warranted her direct involvement had been unknowingly delegated, impeding her effectiveness.

In response, a dual-pronged strategy took shape. First, a realignment of tasks breathed new life into her role, liberating her from the operational quagmire. Second, a targeted refinement of delegation strategies safeguarded her strategic responsibilities while empowering her team to excel in their specialized realms.

The transformation was resounding. Angie shed the burden, reclaiming her stride with newfound confidence. The clarity she regained illuminated her interactions, and her department rekindled its momentum. Her journey underscores the pivotal role of recalibration and astute delegation in leadership growth.

Angie's narrative is a testament to adaptive leadership—where strategy, communication, and empowerment craft a story of resilience and triumph. Her tale invites us to align tasks with roles and wield delegation as a tool for growth.

* * *

CHAPTER 7
RESOLVING CONFLICTS WITH RELATIONSHIP MANAGEMENT

M anaging a team often involves resolving conflicts, no matter how rare. A leader must realize their role in mediating disputes. Understanding the connection between effective leadership and conflict resolution will aid in seeing trouble spots before they escalate and finding workable solutions when they do arise. In this chapter, we'll talk about a leader's role in preventing and resolving conflicts within a team and provide some practical advice for doing so.

Conflict Resolution Strategies for Leaders

Managers have the difficult task of resolving workplace conflicts arising from differences of opinion, personal grudges, and misunderstandings. Although it may be challenging, conflict management can lead to beneficial results. Leaders can employ techniques including encouraging open communication, addressing personal grievances, and establishing a culture of understanding and teamwork to prevent conflict from developing and producing rifts among team members. Learn more about the following tactics:

Open Communication

Open communication promotes straightforward discussion of issues in a practical conflict management approach. Executives need to foster a workplace culture of trust and safety by encouraging their teams to listen to one another and share their ideas actively.

To communicate during conflict:

- Pose clarifying questions to the parties engaged in the conflict, such as "Can you be more specific about what is frustrating you?" or "What questions do you have that aren't being answered?"
- Insist that they give the other person a hearing and an opportunity to explain their perspective.
- If things are getting heated, have everyone take a break.
- Schedule a meeting the next day to process the information and debate the three points in writing.

Assertive Communication

Assertiveness is an effective tool for managing conflicts. Solution-proposing and conversational forward momentum are also important components of effective communication. When using direct speech to end a disagreement:

- Establish ground rules for potentially contentious team meetings and talks. For example, you may say, "We'll give everyone five minutes to air their grievances, and then we'll vote democratically on the best course of action."
- Avoid letting issues fester. Ask for specifics when others express anger, offense, or disagreement.

- Pay attention to body language. Ask individuals how they feel when you detect subtle changes in their body language or the place's ambiance.
- It's important to have difficult conversations, even if they make people uncomfortable, and to bring everyone back down to earth when tempers flare.
- Encourage people to express their interpretations of others' words, thoughts, and deeds using the "I feel like" format.

Active Listening

When you actively listen, you focus on gaining comprehension. Feelings might get in the way when discussing a dispute and finding a solution. Such behavior does not bring people together to solve issues but deepens their divide.

To minimize conflicts:

Call for a moment of silence so everyone can process the presented information. Then, have your team report back what was conveyed.

- Make sure no one is talking over another person.
- Pose inquiries that facilitate the separation of competing perspectives. For example, you could ask, "Okay, so what do you think you can agree on?" Alternatively, "What is it that you two hope to accomplish?"
- First, have them look for a positive aspect of what was stated, and then give them a chance to say something like, "From my perspective," "the way I see it," or "My understanding is..." You must set an example to convince your team to adopt this behavior independently.

Stress Management

The adverse effects of these physiological reactions on stressful events can be mitigated with regular stress management practices. Therefore, the likelihood of a happy outcome increases compared to letting the conflict worsen.

To manage stress:

- Working out, going for a walk, or some other form of physical activity
- Engaging in a moving meditation like yoga, tai chi, or qi gong (which promote mental peace by emphasizing slow, controlled motion)
- Doing box breathing or other breathing exercises. To accomplish this, hold a four-second breath, and then take a four-second breath out. Do it three times.
- Conferring with people who are there for you emotionally, whether they be friends, family, a therapist, a life coach, or a mentor

Collaboration

The ability to work together effectively is an essential tool for resolving conflicts and fostering consensus. Leaders need to share the big picture, get people talking, and get them to stop thinking "me" and start thinking "we." Organizations can realize their full potential and overcome competitive mindsets by encouraging collaboration and group decision-making. That can be accomplished through the adoption of a democratic leadership style and the implementation of group decision-making processes.

Compromise

True leaders should be able to find a middle ground. The goal of a compromise is to ensure that all parties involved feel as though they have received a fair share of the cake. Leaders must ensure everyone is happy with the resolution and zero in on where everyone can agree.

Negotiation

There is a difference between negotiation and compromise. While negotiation entails giving and taking, compromise is about working together to find a solution for everyone. For instance, two business owners may agree on the conditions they seek by agreeing to a one-year contract at a lower price than a three-year plan.

To negotiate fairly:

- Inquire into the "non-negotiables" of all parties participating in the decision-making process. They must agree to these conditions before proceeding.
- Use aggressive language to establish your goals and explain how to reach them.
- Be adaptable and willing to give in on details that won't significantly impact the final result.
- Consider the negotiation a challenge that must be met. Involve others whose opinions differ from your own to reach a compromise.

Problem-Solving

There are internal conflicts in decision-making because businesses want to tackle the problems of their consumers, clients, and the world. Teams can lessen friction by adopting a cooperative mentality and working through challenges collaboratively, allowing everyone to contribute to the success of the company's overall objective.

Accountability

Taking full responsibility for one's words, thoughts, and deeds, displaying integrity as a leader, fostering positive connections, and displaying emotional intelligence are all aspects of accountability. Accountability role modeling encourages a sense of modesty and mutual respect among team members, raising everyone's level of self and social awareness.

To take responsibility and to make others take responsibility:

- Have employees sign off on rules and regulations outlining expected conduct before employment.
- If you've said or done something wrong, accept responsibility and stop blaming others. It is most effective to teach accountability by example.
- Normalize failure.
- If tensions rise, you must pause and consider how you will respond. When dealing with disagreement, ask others to do the same.
- The team's existing lines of communication should be re-emphasized.

Conflicts and Their Solutions

Conflict resolution is shown in the examples below. You will learn what conflict resolution skills to employ and how to apply them after reading the following cases:

An Employee Has Difficulty Accepting Criticism

During a one-on-one with their boss, a team member vents their anger and dissatisfaction with their employment. An employee becomes defensive and insists that they are the ones who are the problem when their boss confronts them.

Methods for Addressing and Resolving Conflict

- Open communication
- Assertive communication
- Accountability

Addressing negative attitudes and establishing clear limits requires both open and assertive communication. Stress the importance of feedback in achieving individual, team, and organizational objectives, and stress the importance of respecting and owning one's work.

A fight breaks out between two team members during a meeting

A graphic designer raises an issue during brainstorming that will require the attention of the team's primary copywriter. The writer rejects the proposal, calling it unjust and threatening to notify HR.

Methods for Addressing and Resolving Conflict

- Stress management
- Shifting away from blame and shame
- Compromise

When employees have a heated argument, asking for a second meeting and talking briefly with both parties is best. Inquire about their feelings rather than making assumptions about what's wrong. Work together for the rest of the day to find a middle ground to allow the organization to achieve its goals. HR may need to be brought in if a solution cannot be found through cooperative effort.

There Is No Consensus Among Leaders

The chief executive officer of a corporation is concerned that the terms of the business proposition are unfavorable. The individual leading the negotiations is also overly aggressive and unwilling to compromise. That's the best we can do, and we would only bring it to you if we thought the terms were fair, they tell the CEO.

Practical Advice for Handling Conflict

- Assertive communication
- Collaboration
- Problem-Solving

- Negotiation

Make it clear that the existing terms are unacceptable to you, and suggest working together to discover a solution that works for everyone. It's vital to lay out the problems and ask for suggestions.

Participate in Conflict Resolution Training with Your team
Learning to work through disagreements constructively is essential for the development of all levels of a team. Conflict can be harnessed rather than equalized through the promotion of constructive discussion and increased team member involvement. The growth of leaders and the enhancement of corporate operations can result from disseminating conflict management advice to employees and human resources departments.

Relationship Management and Its Importance in Leadership
In leadership, relationships are essential. A successful company leader will leverage their network to collaborate with others and influence decision-makers. Leaders can only unite their followers behind a common goal if they take the time to cultivate strong relationships with them. Managing your team's relationships is crucial. A leader can only effectively construct a unit if they effectively interact with and acquire the trust of the team members. Fundamental relationship management abilities that can aid leaders are listed below.

Assertive Communication
Effective relationship management necessitates the use of aggressive language. It's the power to convey and discuss one's innermost sentiments and beliefs. Assertive communication is crucial for leaders to guide their teams effectively.

Making one's argument without dismissing the other party's sentiments and viewpoints sets great leaders apart from good ones.

Decision Making

Both efficient relationship management and effective leadership may be boiled down to one thing: good decision-making. A relationship might suffer from hasty or incorrect decision-making. The same is true for teams: bad decisions can have devastating effects.

It's tough to win over everyone, no matter how hard you try. Convincing others to support a choice they initially disagree with is integral to the decision-making process. On the other hand, people adept at managing their relationships are also adept at making sound decisions, ultimately leading to stellar leadership. Leadership and rational decision-making go hand in hand.

Adaptability

Leaders who adapt to changing circumstances in their relationships are more likely to succeed. Leaders need flexibility to deal with external stakeholders, internal stakeholders, and the many voices inside their teams. This ability is crucial for managing relationships and getting the best results for everyone involved.

Problem-Solving

Problem-solving is essential to relationship management because conflicts arise in all relationships. The ability to think critically and solve problems is a hallmark of effective leadership.

Mediation as a Tool for Resolving Conflict in the Workplace

Two team members' tensions boil over into an open conflict while you're serving as the project manager. This incident initially had no apparent bearing on the project, but now everyone is worried. Today's workplaces are intricate webs of competing ideals, priorities, and assumptions. Although mediation is an effective method for resolving problems, it is crucial to consider when to use it and provide a detailed guide.

What Is Meditation?

Mediation is a form of conflict management in which an outside, neutral party assists group members in working out their differences. The goal is to defuse tense situations before they can cause serious harm in the workplace. It's a less rigid and more malleable alternative to traditional procedures like reprimands and appeals. Follow these guidelines for more effective mediation:

Establish the Ground rules

To begin, schedule individual meetings with all involved parties to review ground rules and expectations. If neither party is willing to mediate, the process will fail. Set some guidelines for the following steps. Among these are encouraging everyone to think of potential answers or ideas ahead of time, encouraging attentive listening, and discouraging interruptions. You must earn both parties' confidence so they can speak freely and honestly with you and one another.

Discuss everything openly and honestly with each person

Locate a private area where team members can talk freely without interruption. Listen carefully, ask clarifying questions, and think about what they have to say. Pay attention to body language and utilize emotional intelligence to determine what's bothering the other person. Fear, sadness, wrath, and the desire for vengeance are all normal reactions. The important thing is not to stifle them. Inquire about the participants' expectations for the mediation and emphasize that the goal is not an individual win but a workable solution that satisfies all parties.

Explore the Issues together

To discuss the disagreement, you should call a meeting. Kick things off on a good note by reiterating the rules, providing a brief overview of the problem, and noting where there is consensus and dispute. Foster honest dialogue, equal time, and compassion. Bring the discourse back to the core issue if the other person becomes defensive or angry.

Negotiate and compromise

Meetings should shift their focus from the past to the future and seek common ground. Gain momentum and trust by fixing problems promptly. Promote creative problem-solving and a win-win approach to negotiations. If you think an idea is out of line, check with the proposer to see whether they concur.

Create a Written agreement

Keep detailed notes and draft a legally binding agreement throughout mediation sessions, including SMART (Specific, Measurable, Achievable, Relevant, and Time-bound) goals. Keep the wording objective, read it aloud to check for comprehension, and consider having both parties sign it. That makes the decision more official and binding but could also undercut the mediation process's more relaxed tone.

Get Some closure

The mediation session must now end. Provide participants copies of the approved statement and outline your expectations for their return to work.

Set aside some time to discuss potential roadblocks to enforcing the agreement and brainstorm solutions before moving forward. Briefly summarize what will happen next, assure both parties of your availability as a mediator, and express gratitude for their assistance.

Cope with Conflict and Keep Your Workplace Happy

Leadership requires making tough calls and speaking on behalf of the company, yet discussing conflicts can be fraught with difficulty. Managers should stress the positive effects of healthy competition on creativity and development. Managing disagreements is essential for a flourishing workplace where problems don't fester or grow. Managing conflicts is more than just a must for success in this role. To keep things positive in the workplace, consider these methods for conflict resolution:

Don't make choices based on how you feel

When people have strong feelings about something, it might activate the sympathetic nervous system and cause them to go into "fight or flight" mode. Step away from the situation, take a few deep breaths, and focus on the present moment to help resolve problems. That makes it possible to think more clearly and react more effectively.

Preventing Conflict by Recognizing It Early

Although conflict is unavoidable, it can be avoided or mitigated if preventative measures are taken. You must clarify the situation if a team member is unsure of their assignment. When instructions are vague, tensions grow. Team members should check in in pairs to ensure they are on the same page. We need to talk to each other.

Consult with both sides and then convene a meeting

Discuss honestly, establish ground rules, and ensure active listening to help parties resolve their issue in an impartial context. If talking it out doesn't work, try negotiating an agreement. Detailed implementation procedures must be documented once a compromise or optimal solution has been identified.

Choose Your battles

We know now that conflicts will arise; the question is whether or not we should invest time and effort into resolving them. The Harvard Business Review recommends using a scale from 1 to 10, with 10 representing the most critical issue. If the total is less than six, discard it. It may be worthwhile to address a sub-six issue if you believe it has the potential to balloon into a major one. Pay attention to the obstacles preventing your organization and team from succeeding.

Monitor and Follow Up

It's essential to keep an eye on things after resolving a quarrel. Team members' tensions have yet to be entirely handled, or the issue must be fixed from all angles. You'll have to tweak the answer to make it work as you envision.

You must do what is right, not what is convenient, even if some are unhappy with your choice.

Change Your Thinking: Confrontation Can Be A Learning Experience

Create a work environment where dissent is celebrated. It would be best if you didn't want your staff to feel that they can't voice their concerns for fear of contributing to a "negative" workplace atmosphere.

Resolving conflicts shouldn't be viewed as a burden. The best leaders see this as a chance to advance the company's mission, bond the workforce closer together, and spark creativity.

Gabriel's Story

While working for a highly esteemed mass food service company, I encountered a scenario that is all too familiar in the corporate world. Albert, who had long held the warehouse manager position, had been promoted to a higher role. Simultaneously, Gabriel had recently taken the reins as the new warehouse manager, succeeding Albert. As anticipated, Gabriel faced initial challenges in his new position due to a lack of comprehensive onboarding, leading to some instability in processes and teamwork within the warehouse area. This instability had a ripple effect, compromising the efficiency and precision of order preparation for other departments.

Albert's discerning eye quickly picked up on these deficiencies. He frequently marched into my office, candidly expressing his concerns about Gabriel's perceived negligence and inefficiency. On occasion, even during the Daily Direction Settings (DDS) meetings, Albert would publicly highlight the shortcomings he had observed. Albert's ability to identify these issues stemmed from his firsthand experience in the same role he had held before his promotion. These criticisms, though accurate in their observations, had a detrimental impact on Gabriel's confidence, leaving him questioning his capabilities in his new position.

The straightforward solution might have involved heeding Albert's complaints and disciplining Gabriel for his apparent underperformance, given the accuracy of Albert's assessments. However, such an approach would have yielded no benefits. Addressing Albert's grievances without a strategic plan would not contribute to the overall improvement of the warehouse operations.

Taking a proactive stance, I embarked on a collaborative journey with Albert. The objective was to channel his concerns into opportunities for enhancement and deliver them constructively. The next step involved Albert directly communicating his insights to Gabriel. Together with Gabriel and his team, they devised actionable strategies to rectify the inconsistencies they identified in their work.

Surprisingly, Albert's communication style transformed significantly. Not only did he become more effective in conveying his points, but he also displayed heightened empathy and understanding towards Gabriel. Albert was now adept at placing himself in Gabriel's shoes, leveraging his own experience to guide him in optimizing the efficiency of the warehouse area. This approach bolstered Gabriel's decision-making self-assurance and fostered a sense of support. Within a short time, the improvements were palpable, reflected in a noticeable reduction in issues raised during the DDS meetings.

* * *

CHAPTER 8
STIMULATING INNOVATION THROUGH CREATIVITY AND CALCULATED RISKS

There has been a rise in the term creative leadership and innovation leadership. According to polls and studies, the absence of original thought is the biggest problem with new hiring. Similarly, originality is regarded as vital in a leader. Creative leaders can think of and implement novel solutions during structural complexity or change.

When everything around them changes, and there are no clear solutions, these leaders can give their teams a sense of direction and focus. These are the types of leaders who not only accept but seek out the inherent uncertainty in their environments. That benefits the company, the individual, society, and the environment.

LEADERSHIP AND THE ART OF INNOVATION

Leadership Strategies that Make Use of Creativity

Leadership requires imagination since it facilitates the introduction of novel techniques and approaches in the workplace.

What does innovative leadership entail?

Leadership that demonstrates creativity fosters new ways of thinking and motivates employees to solve problems. By praising participation in non-traditional ways, leaders can inspire the creation of novel company strategies, improve working conditions, and develop interpersonal and communication abilities.

What makes innovative thinking so vital for leaders?

You and your team may forge new paths to professional success with exemplary, innovative leadership. Here are some more arguments in favor of innovative leadership:

- Encourages innovative problem-solving. When faced with a challenge, your team will respond better to leadership, enabling them to think outside the box.
- A leader who fosters creativity can help you promote a supportive and inclusive workplace by encouraging employees to share their ideas and build relationships with one another via the creative process.
- It assists in adapting to changing circumstances by allowing you to develop novel solutions that align with established standards in your field. Your ability to think creatively makes you more resilient to disruptions in the workplace.
- The capacity to think outside the box and develop novel solutions to problems can positively impact a company's bottom line.

Methods for fostering originality in a managerial role

If you want to be an effective leader who makes use of creativity, consider the following ways:

Discover Educational Opportunities for Your Career
Develop a varied viewpoint and approach to creativity through learning from various sources, such as online courses, innovation seminars, and interviews with mentors. Connect with other heads of departments to swap ideas on how to inspire innovation in the workplace.

Work on your leadership skills
Adopt the mindset of an innovative leader by trying new things in the workplace. Increase your self-assurance by challenging assumptions, seeking clarification, and exploring new avenues. Keep a journal regularly to observe your thoughts and gauge your development. You can highlight these essential traits of a creative leader in your work:

- Making things happen. Innovative leaders change procedures and foster an upbeat atmosphere in the workplace.
- The most innovative leaders are those who trust their gut when handling pressing issues and significant decisions. Integrate your instincts and thoughts with rational approaches using your imagination.
- Exuding assurance. Show that you trust yourself to express your opinions with others constructively.
- Motivating individual achievement entails recognizing personal growth drivers, gaining exposure to alternative methods of handling professional obligations, and establishing aspirational objectives.

Integrate differing points of view
Join forces with people of different backgrounds, experiences, and positions to spark new ideas. Motivate employees to take initiative, solve problems, and share their unique viewpoints

on company matters. Motivate your employees to take the initiative and share their thoughts.

Incorporate narrative approaches

Nothing beats a good story to build a strong team and strengthen bonds. To improve your storytelling skills, observe those around you, inquire about their interests at work, and watch entertaining online videos. Improve your team's communication ability by paying attention to structure and exciting details. Some aspects of storytelling that can be observed and included in professional discourse are listed below:

- Suspense: Think about the techniques the storyteller uses to build suspense.
- Structure: Analyze how the narrator sets the scene, conveys their perspective on the matter, and then offers a solution.
- Imagery: Pay close attention to the visual details of the story and how they enrich and complicate the material you absorb.

Think of multiple options

Start a new project by having a group discussion and letting ideas flow freely. Make changes to the plan to fit the company's requirements and the available resources. Make use of online whiteboards and papers for collaborative brainstorming.

Refine your ideas

Creative thinking requires honing and expanding upon fundamental concepts. Select feasible alternatives and fill in the information in a new project. Find the links between your thoughts and formulate an approach. Combining traditional sales methods with social media efforts is one example of successfully using sales strategies on these channels.

Help others by imparting your wisdom to them
Participate in community events to learn about innovative leadership practices, contribute your methods, and get input from others. Develop your abilities and think of creative ways to use your knowledge. Participate in panel discussions and give speeches to build your profile as an innovative thought leader.

Leadership advice that emphasizes the importance of imagination
Think about the following advice on how to be a more creative leader:

- Keep an open mind. Instead of rigidly adhering to established procedures, try something new with your next endeavor after learning something useful. Being adaptable and willing to take risks can help you find more effective methods of reaching your objectives.
- Make creative thinking a regular part of your workday by setting aside time to plan how to inspire innovation among your staff. Pick an hour or two when you will be able to continue.
- Keep a cool head by having a good time with your team. Plan engaging activities and have stimulating chats. Creative thinking typically occurs when people are at ease.
- Keep trying new things. If one of your creative ideas backfires or needs to improve, promise to continue trying until you find the solution.

Leadership with imagination is essential to increasing output and growing a business. It calls for the adoption of novel organizational strategies. The following describes how leaders can learn and grow, inspiring innovation and creativity in their teams and the organizations they represent.

Ways to Develop Your Creative Leadership Skills

The leader and the organization can significantly benefit from embracing their inner artists. Leaders can lose their ability to inspire their teams and contribute novel ideas when tasked with managing the business and other responsibilities. The following six innovative leadership development methods will guarantee your continued professional growth.

Continue to Educate yourself

Being a visionary leader requires a commitment to lifelong learning. Strategies for innovative leadership in the work-place can be learned from various educational articles and courses. Leaders should consult with more seasoned colleagues and team members to hone their abilities.

Attend Industry events

Seminars and workshops focusing on teamwork, leadership, and management are standard components of corporate training programs. Attending conferences significantly improves your leadership skills, inspires your team, and boosts productivity.

Trust the Group and Help Them Develop

A team can function as an extension of an innovative leader, aiding in decision-making and problem-solving. Giving employees and executives a lot of leeway to make their own decisions is a great way to foster innovation and creativity. Leaders who enable innovation by depending on their teams can concentrate on the larger picture and develop fresh concepts, prototypes, and methods.

Develop Thought leadership

Having credibility as an innovative leader requires establishing oneself as an expert in one's field. Sharing groundbreaking concepts and tracking their development might help you stand out as a creative leader. There are many ways to establish yourself as an industry leader, but here are just a few:

- Webinar Presentations
- Talking at Conferences and Conventions
- Participating in Industry Groups
- Discussing findings on social networking sites like LinkedIn
- Developing articles for your site
- Seek opportunities to contribute as a guest blogger on other websites.
- Teach others and serve as an example of innovative leadership in any of these roles.

Allow Yourself Some Pre-Planned Time for Innovation

Leaders who are also creative need downtime to think things through. They need to think strategically and imaginatively. Companies like Google succeed in creativity because they give their employees much freedom and encourage them to speak their minds. Clarity and time away from the company's routine can be found in periods of silence, physical activity, time spent outside, and meditation.

Have Fun

Participating in unplanned outings as a team or with colleagues at work is a great way to encourage open discussion and new ideas. Employees and peers benefit from the increased productivity and fresh ideas fostered by the lack of rigidity. The mood and vitality of a leader who is also creative are contagious.

Leaders Should Take Risks, Even If They Could Fail

As a manager, I have had the opportunity to network with leaders from various fields. One advice I received as a leader was not to fear failure. Success cannot be achieved without first experiencing failure; failure is the only way to grow and develop. Leaders willing to take risks and learn from missteps are more likely to succeed. To encourage leaders to take calculated risks, I employ a five-step methodology.

Step 1: 'Fire Bullets, Then Cannonballs

The items in the bullets are all relatively inexpensive, safe, and unobtrusive. The risks from cannonballs are significantly higher. I only suggest people take a massive risk after first trying smaller ones. It would be best to ease into taking risks by starting with low-stakes ones. You should know how much danger you will face and act accordingly without second-guessing yourself.

Step 2: Act, Assess, And Adjust

Move forward and evaluate what's happening. The question, "Are we all on the same page?" must be asked. Although it wasn't created with business in mind, this method has helped me immensely in my educational leadership and business endeavors.

Step 3: Go Ahead, Fail!

To fail is to gain valuable experience. Many people avoid taking chances because they worry about making mistakes. It's okay to try and fail. You will continue to develop as long as you take the time to reflect on and correct your actions. Defeat is but a stepping stone on the road to victory. This time, the catch is that you must draw wisdom from the experience. You are more likely to try new things when you do not fear making mistakes.

Step 4: Keep an open mind and avoid becoming too attached to anything

The best idea will win if you're open to anything and not attached to anything. Our limited willingness to take chances is often due to our fixed ideas about the world. This fact encourages one to adopt a more daring attitude. You can quickly try new ideas when you are not committed to one.

Your beliefs or methods change if you're willing to keep an open mind. Consistency is a hallmark of a strong leader, but it can backfire if you allow yourself to become "consistently consistent" instead of evolving.

Step 5: Be authentic

Authenticity can only be attained through taking risks, whether it is a risk to better oneself, commit, or reveal one's true self to others. Take these chances, and you'll build trust, vulnerability, and the courage to try and fail. Taking risks and being open to the unexpected helps you learn and develop as a person without losing sight of your ultimate goals. Leaders must be willing to take these risks to succeed and flourish in their positions.

Why Setbacks Are Essential to Progress in Innovation

Appliance breakdowns and technological glitches are two examples of problems that might arise due to inevitable human error. There is a reciprocal relationship between innovation and failure. However, many businesses have trouble embracing their inventive spirit because of the potential repercussions of making mistakes. The following passage explores the reasons behind people's avoidance of failure, strategies for cultivating an environment that embraces it, and its significance in the creative process.

The Taboo Of Failure

The development of the lightbulb by Thomas Edison is only one example of how failure may lead to success in science, industry, and other fields. It took Edison 2,000 tries to find a suitable carbon filament, and he built on the labor of many failed inventors over 50 years to create the modern light bulb.

Others, like the Wright Brothers and Edison, made mistakes before achieving a remarkable achievement. It only works if an experiment or project provides the desired results. But that's sometimes a terrible thing, too. There is no shame in pausing an investigation to try a different strategy later as long as you analyze the reasons for its failure.

The Art of Accepting Failure Within Your Company

It is typically more productive to approach complex tasks from various directions. More perspectives increase the likelihood of finding a novel solution to a problem. Creating the proper conditions for teamwork is essential. When working together:

- No one individual or group is in charge of idea generation.
- Team members regularly discuss their thoughts to build on each other's ideas.
- The new concept is nurtured while incorporating the lessons learned from earlier statements.

Make mistakes while trying out new ideas

We only have a little opportunity to grow when things are going smoothly. It's time to start letting good ideas fail in tests. The more you learn about each possibility, the closer you will come to a unique answer. To make this work, you must establish a mindset that recognizes and embraces setbacks. Letting your team know that falling is acceptable and essential to reaching your goals would be best. The best way to learn from their mistakes is for others to share their discoveries.

Produce prototypes and physical artifacts using the same methods consistently

To find a solution, it helps to have as much information as possible regarding the issue at hand. Doing so lets you establish worthwhile objectives and guarantee that your answer will be practical in light of your users, business goals, and limits. You can determine whether or not a concept is promising based on the facts gathered using a consistent methodology.

Innovation is a Mess—Learn to Love It

Only about a few years ago, most businesses needed to use video conferencing more. Despite initial setbacks, Loom's founding team remained committed to the company's objectives and grew the business into a $1.5 billion market leader. If you want to fail with grace, you need to train your team to do so. Failure is not a certainty but rather an opportunity to learn and improve for the next attempt. Individuals can take chances and advance their ideas by accepting failure as an inevitable part of the invention process.

Lead Your Team by Challenging Assumptions in Six Easy Steps

Professionals were able to realize their full potential and propel their teams forward by adhering to the following six guiding principles:

Ultimately, Your Achievements Are Measured By How You See them.

What constitutes success for one person may differ for another, regardless of how much money they bring in. Developing one's idea of success, independent of social norms, is liberating and empowering. The courage to attempt something new and push ourselves can improve outcomes. We must challenge ourselves and be careful not to overreact or jump to conclusions about the future. We can only know how anything will turn out if we try it or take a leap of faith.

Leverage the Forces of Transition

Life is constantly shifting, and adjusting to those shifts ultimately matters. Leaders must show compassion for their teams and engage in one-on-one interactions to learn about their unique experiences and opinions. That paves the way for them to embrace the shift and provide exceptional skills and perspectives. Leaders must also address issues, including resistance to change, confusion, and poor communication. Trust and teamwork are essential to any project's success, and effective personnel management is a prerequisite. Human resource management is the key to a successful transition.

Push the envelope

To push the limits, you must encourage your team members to use their strengths and celebrate their successes. Taking this tack helps to create a group dynamic in which everyone feels safe enough to share their true selves. Leaders who push the limits do more than allow their teams to make the most of their talents; they actively encourage it.

Create a Culture of vulnerability

Recognizing limitations and encouraging openness are hallmarks of a culture of vulnerability in the workplace. Leaders should model these characteristics to inspire their teams to adopt them. Leaders and followers alike can build trust and transparency by being honest about their shortcomings, leading to more efficient mission execution if only the leaders would model such behavior. A more united and efficient team emerges when an environment encourages open conversations about challenges, solutions, and accomplishments.

Learn to Accept Setbacks as Part of the Learning Process

If businesses want to grow, they must accept that failure is integral to learning. There is no way around making choices or avoiding setbacks. Adopting a growth mindset, setting lofty goals, and implementing novel ideas necessitates conquering obstacles.

The trick is to take risks without allowing the prospect of failure to paralyze you

Such a frame of mind will keep you stuck in place, unable to change your current situation. The truth is that no company, no sports team, and no sector of the economy stands still.

Keeping things as they are will lead to failure as your rivals advance.

Tailor Your Leadership

Each of these guidelines hinges on getting to know your team members personally so you can learn how they define success and what they can bring to the table. You will go far as a leader if you take the time to get to know each member of your team on an individual basis.

The benefits of scheduling individual meetings with each team member outweigh the time commitment.

Benefits of a Diverse Workforce in a Collaborative Culture

Female CEOs make up only 4.1% of the Fortune 500. It can be challenging to increase workplace diversity and inclusion, but a culture of cooperation pays off in increased productivity, creativity, and customer satisfaction. Collaborative groups naturally become very multi-ethnic in their membership. Here are five guiding principles managers need to adopt to foster an inclusive and collaborative environment:

- **Give everyone a voice:** The lack of a forum for employees' opinions is a significant drawback to top-down work cultures. Supportive environments, fertile ground for innovation, and cultivating younger employees can result from open communication and acknowledging varied viewpoints. Removing barriers, boosting confidence, and raising fulfillment can all result from recognizing and allowing employees to express their thoughts without pressure.
- **Be transparent:** Employees are likely to stay with an honest company that is open to them. Employees can create an inclusive culture and encourage teamwork by learning the company's

processes, making decisions, and planning for the future.

- **Try to find a leader who can inspire teamwork:** Diversity in hiring is essential, but so is keeping that talent. Employees typically leave a manager rather than a company. It's critical for staff retention to have managers that workers enjoy working with. Fair, supportive managers who recognize and provide feedback can benefit job performance and advancement prospects.

- **Have your employees' backs:** Women and minorities suffer from a lack of diversity among their role models. Organizations can improve access for all members of society by fostering growth and assisting their staff. Especially in oppressive contexts, this helps people feel safe enough to open up and grow.

- **Remove barriers:** Professional barriers exist for some minorities, especially women. Changing people's minds about these stereotypes can help create a more inclusive workplace. Women's empowerment and the reduction of gender biases can result from the implementation of legislation that allows parental leave without detrimental effects on employment. Fostering trust and promoting greater diversity are other benefits of encouraging men to take on caring tasks.

Improving diversity in the workplace is an ongoing commitment that will only happen with effort. A diverse and collaborative culture results from investment in time, training, and reinforcement, and there is always potential for improvement, whether starting from scratch or continuing to evolve existing policies.

· · ·

Claire's Story

Throughout my career, I've come to appreciate the pivotal role innovation plays in propelling businesses forward, particularly in the face of challenging operational or financial circumstances. A crucial lesson I've learned is that micromanagement is a formidable foe to innovation. When we attempt to tightly control every aspect and dictate each move to our team, we inadvertently suppress the potential for groundbreaking ideas to emerge. It's a reminder of the need to position capable individuals in fitting roles strategically and offer ongoing guidance through monitoring and coaching. It's our responsibility to establish the "what" of a departmental goal and allow our team the space to astonish us with their ingenuity in devising the "how." It's a recognition that, no matter how skilled we are individually, the collective wisdom and creativity of the team far surpass our own. In this context, fostering an environment where ideas can flourish is paramount. Our role then becomes one of refining and molding these ideas within the framework we provide, ensuring they remain aligned with the overarching objective, preventing them from veering off course or the team from losing sight of their focus.

Claire's transformative journey exemplifies this principle. She took a once daily, last-minute production process and metamorphosed it into a streamlined volume production system, incorporating freezing techniques to ensure on-time orders and minimize quality concerns. This metamorphosis was orchestrated in the context of a catering company grappling with persistent challenges in order fulfillment. Frequently, customers placed orders with scant 24-hour notice, piling on pressures related to workforce, raw materials, and the potential for errors. Remarkably, this operation persisted for over two decades.

When the task of collaborating with this company's managers fell to me, my initial skepticism stemmed from my unfamiliarity with culinary arts. My attempts at baking bread at home consistently yielded charred results—I'm not joking! However, I realized their untapped potential reservoir upon engaging with the team, rendering my culinary prowess irrelevant. A pool of untapped ideas surfaced, stifled by the sentiment of "that's how things have always been done." Our sessions to mitigate grievances and enhance operational efficiency became incubators for novel activities, strategies, procedures, and methods. The shared objective was to break free from the confines of existing paradigms burdened with dissatisfaction and meager profitability.

In this process, Claire emerged as a beacon of transformation. After harboring an idea for years, she unveiled a novel concept: a shift from spontaneous production to a standardized menu, frozen and brimming with customer choices. These meals, ready for reheating in ovens, revolutionized meal preparation. Yet, this innovation demanded investments, backing from the quality team to ensure adherence to food standards, and a production team willing to shift focus from daily tasks to inventory replenishment. The proposition underwent meticulous scrutiny, revealing remarkable benefits —enhanced customer service and streamlined production costs. This compelling case made securing approval for the initiative a breeze, propelling it into swift implementation.

* * *

CHAPTER 9
THE POWER OF 21: HOT TIPS FOR EMPOWERING LEADERSHIP

Advice from seasoned managers can help your company run more efficiently by coordinating your staff and using your resources better. Effective delegation, developing leadership abilities, and providing sound advice are just a few examples. The purpose of these guidelines is to encourage a culture where meeting the needs of customers and developing team members are equally valued. Management talents, leadership styles, and coaching philosophies are all analogous to these management pointers. You can also use these suggestions to enhance your management abilities.

The foundations of good management are teamwork, growth, and open communication. The following advice can help you develop into a competent manager. So, shall we?

Hunger to learn

Keep an open mind about expanding your managerial abilities. Don't repeat the blunder of more seasoned managers who are too entrenched in their ways to see alternatives. It would be best if you were flexible and open to new ways of doing things and using technology as it develops. You've put in a lot of time and effort to earn this promotion, and you're an expert in your industry. However, this may leave you needing to improve your leadership abilities. Learn as much as you can from your coworkers. You'll be able to settle into your new role more quickly.

Delegate Effectively

You can't just give assignments to your coworkers and expect good results if you want to delegate effectively. Instead, you should evaluate current responsibilities and workloads to find an employee who can complete this task on schedule and with the necessary skills. Delegation can also mean finding people on your team with the expertise you need to do the job. This move furthers the professional development of a team member while also helping you finish a project. Time management, skill distribution, and staff development are all crucial components of effective delegation.

Work on Establishing Rapport

A recent study discovered that employees are more motivated to produce their best work when their managers trust them. As a result, earning people's trust should be a priority for any manager. You get access to one-on-one conferences with each of your direct reports. Learn about their professional goals and how you can help during this meeting. If you invest in your employees' careers, they will invest in your company. Trust and credibility are built on a foundation of openness and honesty. It's essential to consider the team's perspective when making decisions. You may encourage others to take action by sharing what you're learning and your progress. If everyone on the team feels safe enough to express their opinions honestly, it will be easier to build trust.

Develop your Leadership skills

Although they require separate skill sets, "leadership" and "management" are often used interchangeably. You were promoted because you have demonstrated managerial qualities, including problem-solving, organization, and delegation. After being promoted to manager, you should also enhance your leadership abilities. Leaders typically exhibit traits like emotional intelligence, interpersonal understanding, and persistence to inspire their followers to work toward a common goal. While only some successful managers have leadership skills, the best ones do.

Make a Plan to Evaluate Results from the Past

The company's growth and shortcomings can only be monitored if regular, accurate evaluations of team members' progress and output are carried out. An annual one-on-one with each employee is an excellent opportunity to review their growth, recognize their successes, and identify areas for improvement. Employees greatly benefit from performance reviews since they become aware of their manager's appreciation for their hard work.

Establish the Promotion Criteria

Team members are likelier to put forth maximum effort when they clearly know what is expected of them and what they need to do to be considered for a promotion. Promotions may be contingent on team members' meeting specific criteria, such as the ones listed below:

- Maintain regular punctuality.
- Outstanding evaluations of performance
- Qualities of a good leader
- Highest standards of quality
- Willingness to take on more obligations

Managers who provide a clear route to promotion inspire their staff to work hard.

Learn to Cope with Difficult Circumstances

Tense interactions between coworkers account for an average of three hours of American workers' time each week. It's human nature to avoid arguments for fear of making a subordinate angry. However, the situation may get even more dire if no action is taken. It is essential to learn conflict resolution skills on the job. It's crucial to show compassion for team members' worries and listen to them carefully. Finding answers and resolving difficulties requires respecting coworkers' feelings and understanding their points of view.

Recognize the Relationship shift

An increase in tension is frequently associated with changes in working relationships. A promotion could put you in charge of people who were once in your position. Finding common ground between boss and buddy can be difficult but essential. Avoid letting your feelings get in the way of good judgment when sharing confidential information with someone with whom you have a close connection. As a result, it's important to discuss potential changes with your team and earn their confidence before making any big moves.

Offer Professional advice

Each team member can benefit from the manager's potential provision of professional development opportunities. Setting up one-on-one sessions with your team members is a fantastic way to learn about their professional goals and impart any advice you believe might help them achieve them. Provide them with work that will advance their careers.

Assist Workers in Grasping the Mission and Values of the company

A good manager effectively conveys organizational objectives, assigns tasks to employees, and maps out strategies for achieving those objectives. A skilled manager would explain why these tasks are so important in detail. If everyone on your team understands the end goal, they'll be more invested in their duties. One of the most important things you can do as a manager is boost morale, which has been shown to affect productivity positively.

Show Empathy

Effective management relies on empathy because it places a premium on work and people's emotional well-being. Empathetic managers collaborate with their undervalued or overworked staff to discover viable alternatives. When times are good, such as fresh career opportunities, they make themselves available. Managers whose employees feel comfortable sharing their emotions report higher job satisfaction and productivity levels.

Maintain Consciousness When communicating

Managers must be able to communicate with their teams effectively. The first step is to create open communication channels for issues and concerns by delegating duties and explaining their value to staff. By establishing and maintaining reliable communication channels, teams can ensure no questions, comments, or suggestions slip through the cracks. Team members can evaluate their progress toward their objectives and take corrective measures by setting up and maintaining open lines of communication. It benefits everyone when people can easily express their wants and desires to one another.

Make Sure Your Goals Are Specific and Reachable

In a recent survey, 42% of workers named uncertainty the most stressful aspect of their professions. Make your team's lives easier by providing them with clear, actionable goals and deadlines when allocating tasks. The first step in giving precise instructions and evaluation criteria is developing SMART goals, which are specific, measurable, achievable, relevant, and time-bound. This function makes it easier to brief employees on what's expected of them. One strategy for managers to better manage their time is to set realistic goals.

Ask for feedback

Managers can motivate employees by soliciting feedback on their management style. Since sincere criticism cannot be punished, they should not do so. These channels can send feedback on events, initiatives, and employees' performance instantly. Support your team with anonymous feedback tools. Managers should respond positively to input since constructive criticism is not meant to be hurtful. The purpose is to strengthen collaboration and increase productivity in the workplace. One productive use of management meetings is to solicit employee input.

Find a happy medium between individual success and team success

It's easy for managers to lose sight of the finer points when they're focused on the big picture. It's easy to lose sight of the fact that every team member needs to perform at a high level for the group to succeed. Maintaining equilibrium requires a commitment to open communication and collaboration among team members. You can also make sure that the roles everyone plays serve the team's overall goals. If you want to help your team succeed, explain how each member's role relates to the comprehensive plan. This strategy will motivate every employee and drive your team to success.

Maintain Complete transparency

A good manager ensures their staff is well informed to do their tasks properly. They are transparent with their teams, telling them the complete story, ups and downs. Managers should provide regular feedback and updates on company happenings to promote trust and sincerity. Specific feedback is best delivered in one-on-one or company-wide meetings, whereas company-wide meetings and emails help address broad concerns. Transparency and accountability can be maintained through these techniques, which keep employees well informed of their own and the company's development.

Listen More, Talk less

Managers are responsible for ensuring their teams implement management concepts by encouraging clear lines of communication and a culture of offering feedback. Managers who want to be successful should focus more on listening than talking. They need to remember that everyone on the team has their ideas about what does and does not work. Managers can encourage open communication and a more positive work environment by actively listening to and considering the input of their employees.

Motivate your staff

When employees have trouble finishing their work or are just exhausted, it is essential to offer extra motivation. As the manager, you are in an excellent position to inspire your staff. If stressed, you can help them unwind by arranging appreciation events, providing one-on-one guidance, or raising concerns with higher-ups. The goal should be to make the workplace a place where everyone is happy and feels like they can do their best work.

Maintain Consistency

Maintaining high commitment and consistency in dealing with obstacles is essential for effective management. Trust between a manager and their staff can help productivity. Establishing and upholding norms, emphasizing the importance of delegation and updating via one-on-one feedback, and assigning office hours during which suggestions and questions are consistently addressed all contribute to effective management. Because of this uniformity, workers can better meet expectations and contribute to the team's success. When managers set and stick to these standards, they foster an atmosphere of positivity and support for their staff, boosting productivity.

Act as a Leader for your group

Despite the importance of being able to provide constructive feedback and implement disciplinary measures, many managers feel uncomfortable doing so. Instead, you should assume complete responsibility for your team's activities and be prepared to step in whenever necessary. Take a hard stance if you suspect a trusted coworker of withholding facts to keep everyone on the same page. That is essential to taking charge and ensuring everyone contributes to the team's success.

Use Technological resources

Managers can only do their jobs with the help of their teams and modern tools. Efficiency and output can be improved using group chat apps, project management software, and cloud storage services. Meeting preparation is streamlined with collaboration technologies, allowing for efficient follow-up. Managers' productivity is boosted when they have access to a wide range of applications.

The best managers create a work environment that values each employee's unique contributions and needs while prioritizing the company's success. Leaders who succeed keep an open mind and aren't afraid to attempt something new. Therefore, management may increase productivity in the workplace through a variety of means. You can improve as a manager by adopting various management practices.

* * *

If you have not do so. I would love to hear from you!

Your support and review are vital in getting my book to fellow leaders. Please take a moment to leave an Amazon review – it only takes 60 seconds. Scan the QR code below or use the link in your Amazon order if you're outside the listed countries. Here's a quick guide:

Open your mobile camera.
Scan the QR code.
Share your thoughts and rating.

Your feedback means a lot.

Thank you!

AFTERWORD

If you've recently ascended to a management position, mastering the fundamentals of effective leadership is your compass. Grasping the weight of decision-making, adept communication, harmonizing organizational objectives, and adept problem-solving will chart your path to leadership excellence. Do you find yourself grappling with the weight of managerial responsibilities? The journey toward becoming an impactful manager is paved with the refinement of leadership skills. Emerging managers must possess the ability to communicate, make well-founded decisions, inspire teams toward corporate milestones, and devise practical resolutions to challenges.

Even if you confidently embrace the prospect of your new leadership role, taking the plunge can stir up nerves. The transition from being solely accountable for your tasks to shouldering the collective output of a team requires deliberate effort. Yet, the rewards reaped from guiding a team to victory can be substantial. The dance between managers and employees is intricate, demanding astute handling. While anyone can be entrusted with a leadership role, true success belongs to those gifted with innate leadership acumen. This very skill set is what leading firms seek in their quest to identify their successive CEOs.

Management prowess is a skill set that every workforce should cultivate. The World Economic Forum deems adept people management as one of the top 10 skills employers seek today. Gallup's research underscores that companies with capable control see heightened profitability, enhanced productivity, and elevated employee engagement. Regardless of your tenure, whether you're a novice or a seasoned professional, there's always room for improvement in managing people, projects, and resources.

Management profoundly influences a company's bottom line, long-term aspirations, employee productivity, and loyalty. Nearly everyone who's spent substantial time in the workforce can recall clashes with superiors. This commonplace scenario has even inspired numerous Hollywood comedies centered around challenging bosses. Yet, while these comedic spats make for entertaining cinema, they can harm the financial bottom line. According to Gallup, the annual cost of these disputes ranges between $9 to $10 billion.

Navigating the initial steps toward becoming a better leader can be daunting. Feeling a sense of uncertainty and vulnerability when steering your team is natural. Effective management is the cornerstone of organizational success. However, carving out a meaningful impact for new managers can be a steep ascent. The transition into a managerial role could mean embracing a fresh start in a new company or ascending the rungs of your current one.

Companies employ diverse strategies to aid new managers, and each transition presents distinct hurdles. The process requires a period of acclimatization to the new responsibilities. Embracing this role shift necessitates a shift in perspective and a keen eye for the organization's internal mechanisms. The journey often calls for ample guidance as new managers adapt to interacting with employees, upper management, and the public in novel ways.

Effective management has always been challenging, and its complexity has recently amplified. The pace of work has accelerated dramatically, ushering in a shift toward remote and diverse teams. In crisis, 43% of employees report feeling isolated in their roles. The equilibrium between work and personal life is shifting, priorities are realigning, and burnout rates are soaring to unprecedented heights. External forces are also adding fresh challenges to businesses and their management structures. Despite these mounting complexities, it's universally understood that management plays a pivotal role in team (and company) triumph. Gallup's research found that at least 70% of department engagement variance can be attributed to managerial decisions.

A robust management skill set is the cornerstone of a thriving workplace environment. Many businesses are actively refining strategies to support the professional growth of their managers, fine-tuning developmental programs to yield optimal results. As you master the art of guiding others, you'll discover that leadership is exhilarating and fulfilling. It beckons you to expand your horizons and evolve in ways you hadn't envisaged. Each day unfolds as an opportunity to learn, innovate, and make a meaningful impact on the lives of those you hold dear. And simultaneously, you're propelling the company toward its collective aspirations.

Leadership isn't an inherent trait exclusive to exceptional managers. Investing in the growth of your leaders as managers holds the key to unlocking their full potential. This guide is valuable for individuals from newly minted managers to seasoned leaders seeking to refine their skills for unparalleled organizational performance. We've navigated the techniques essential for mastering managerial responsibilities and steering teams through adversity. As demonstrated throughout this guide, I've provided novices and experts with the tools they need to embark on this journey. Best of luck!

* * *